THE PERENNIAL
TRADITION

"Oneing" is an old English word that was used by Lady Julian of Norwich (1342–1416) to describe the encounter between God and the soul. The Rohr Institute proudly borrows the word to express the divine unity that stands behind all of the divisions, dichotomies, and dualisms in the world. We pray and publish with Jesus' words, "that all may be one" (John 17:21).

EDITOR: Vanessa Guerin
ASSISTANT EDITOR: Shirin McArthur
ART DIRECTOR: Nelson Kane
PUBLISHER: The Center for Action and Contemplation

ADVISORY BOARD:
David Benner
James Danaher
Ilia Delio, OSF
Sheryl Fullerton
Marion Küstenmacher

EDITORIAL COMMITTEE:
Richard Rohr, OFM
Alicia Johnson
Vanessa Guerin

Wood engraving by John Steins

Oneing

SPRING 2013 · VOLUME 1 NO. 1

EDITOR'S NOTE

I T IS WITH great enthusiasm that the Center for Action and Contemplation presents the inaugural edition of *Oneing*, the biannual literary journal of the Rohr Institute.

The "Perennial Tradition," the theme of this first issue of *Oneing*, is central to the alternative orthodoxy and teaching methodology of the Institute's Living School for Action and Contemplation. Father Richard Rohr, the school's Academic Dean, offers a clear and concise definition:

> The perennial philosophy or tradition (called by some the Wisdom Tradition) is found as a recurring theme in all of the world's religions and philosophies. Each of these traditions continues to say, in their own way:
>
> • There is a Divine Reality underneath and inherent in the world of things.
> • There is in the human soul a natural capacity, similarity, and longing for this Divine Reality.
> • The final goal of all existence is union with this Divine Reality.

Beginning with Mark Burrows' exquisite translation of Rainer Maria Rilke's prayer from the German and continuing with Ilia Delio's tone-setting article, "Love at the Heart of the Universe," this ancient Wisdom Tradition is masterfully unpacked in these pages of *Oneing* by a roster of esteemed twenty-first century thinkers who together give us an opportunity to expand our understanding of the common core of all faiths. In his epilogue, James Finley offers us the spaciousness to take in all that we have read, sit with it reflectively and become increasingly aware of Divine Reality within our own lives.

I imagine you will return to this issue again and again, revisiting Richard Rohr's overview of the theme and the purpose of Oneing—a publication that we hope will become an essential addition to your library.

Vanessa Guerin,
Editor

CONTRIBUTORS

RICHARD ROHR, OFM, is a Franciscan of the New Mexico Province and the Founding Director of the Center for Action and Contemplation in Albuquerque, New Mexico, home of the Rohr Institute. An internationally recognized author and spiritual leader, Fr. Richard teaches primarily on incarnational mysticism, non-dual consciousness and contemplation, with a particular emphasis on how these affect the social justice issues of our time. Along with many recorded conferences, he is the author of numerous books, including *Everything Belongs: The Gift of Contemplative Prayer, Adam's Return: The Five Promises of Male Initiation, The Naked Now: Learning to See as the Mystics See, Breathing Under Water: Spirituality and the 12 Steps, Falling Upward: A Spirituality for the Two Halves of Life,* and his latest, *Immortal Diamond: The Search for Our True Self.* To learn more about Fr. Richard Rohr and the CAC, visit https://cac.org/.

MARK S. BURROWS, PhD, teaches at the University of Applied Sciences in Bochum, Germany during the academic year. A widely published author whose writings explore matters of spirituality, poetry, and mysticism, he is also well known as a speaker and retreat leader across the United States as well as in Britain, Germany, and Australia. He recently translated a collection of Rainer Maria Rilke's poems, *Prayers of a Young Poet,* and later this year will publish a collection of poems entitled *Psalms* by the German-Iranian poet, SAID. To learn more about Mark Burrows, visit http://www.msburrows.com/about-mark-burrows/.

ILIA DELIO, OSF, PhD, is a Senior Fellow at Woodstock Theological Center, Georgetown University where she concentrates in the area of Science and Religion. She is currently involved in research projects on transhumanism, nature and ecology, and evolutionary theology, especially the writings of Pierre Teilhard de Chardin. She is the author of twelve books and more than sixty publications. Her latest books include *The Unbearable Wholeness of Being: God, Evolution and the Power of Love* and *The Emergent Christ: Exploring the Meaning of Catholic in an Evolutionary Universe*. To learn more about Sr. Ilia Delio, visit http://catholicstudies.georgetown.edu/321406.html.

DAVID G. BENNER, PHD, is a depth psychologist, spiritual guide and author whose life passion has been the understanding and pursuit of awakening and transformation. His most recent books are *Opening to God*, *Soulful Spirituality*, and *Spirituality and the Awakening Self*. To learn more about David Benner, visit www.drdavidgbenner.ca.

JOHN L. ESPOSITO, PHD, is Professor of Religion and International Affairs and of Islamic Studies at Georgetown University, and Founding Director of the Prince Alwaleed Bin Talal Center for Muslim-Christian Understanding in the Walsh School of Foreign Service. John has served as Editor for seven of Oxford's Islamic Encyclopedias and Dictionaries and is the author of more than 45 books and monographs, including *Islamophobia and the Challenge of Pluralism in the 21st Century*, *Unholy War: Terror in the Name of Islam*, *The Islamic Threat: Myth or Reality?*, and *Women in Muslim Family Law*. His books and articles have been translated into more than 35 languages. To learn more about John Esposito, visit http://explore.georgetown.edu/people/jle2/.

DIANA BUTLER BASS, PHD, an author, speaker, and independent scholar specializing in American religion and culture, is currently a Chabraja Fellow with the SeaburyNEXT project at Seabury Western Theological Seminary. She is the author of eight books including *Christianity After Religion: The End of Church and the Birth of a New Spiritual Awakening*, *A People's History of Christianity: the Other Side of the Story*, nominated for a Library of Virginia literary award, and the best-selling *Christianity for the Rest of Us* which was named as one of the best religion books of the year by *Publishers Weekly* and featured in a cover story in *USA Today*. To learn more about Diana Butler Bass, visit http://www.dianabutlerbass.com/.

JOELLE CHASE is Director of Messaging at the Center for Action and Contemplation, helping to craft words that convey the great Mystery (though it can never be fully captured or known through language). She also edits for the online spirituality section of *Spectrum Magazine* and is an occasional blogger and journal-keeper. Joelle's own faith history began in the Seventh-day Adventist church and gradually evolved to a spirituality without labels, a deep resonance with the Perennial Tradition. Joelle

Chase and her husband, Peter Knipper, live on a small urban homestead in Albuquerque, New Mexico where they seek to live more simply and sustainably.

MARY BETH INGHAM, CSJ, PhD, Professor of Philosophical Theology at the Franciscan School of Theology, was part of the organizing committee for the "Quadruple Congress" in celebration of the 8th centenary of John Duns Scotus' death in 2008, and she edited the first volume, *Duns Scotus, Philosopher*, with Oleg Bychkov. Her additional works include *Rejoicing in the Works of the Lord: Beauty in the Franciscan Tradition, La Vie de la Sagesse: Le Stoicisme au Moyen Age, The Harmony of Goodness: Mutuality and Moral Living According to John Duns Scotus, Scotus for Dunces: An Introduction to the Subtle Doctor* and, with Dr. Mechthild Dreyer, *The Philosophical Vision of John Duns Scotus*. To learn more about Sr. Mary Beth Ingham, visit http://fst.edu/faculty/ingham-m/.

JAMES P. DANAHER, PhD, is Professor of Philosophy at Nyack College, Nyack, New York, and the author of *Contemplative Prayer; Jesus after Modernity; Eyes that See, Ears that Hear; Postmodern Christianity and the Reconstruction of the Christian Mind*; and over seventy articles that have appeared in a variety of philosophy and theology journals. To learn more about James Danaher, visit http://www.nyack.edu/files/interviews/James.Danaher.pdf.

ROBERT SARDELLO, PhD, is Co-Director with his wife, Cheryl Sanders-Sardello, PhD, of the School of Spiritual Psychology. He is an independent researcher of spiritual phenomena and the author of numerous books, including *Facing the World with Soul, Love and the World, Freeing the Soul from Fear*, and *The Power of Soul: Living the Twelve Virtues*. Robert Sardello has taught in the USA, England, Ireland, Canada, the Philippines, Holland and Australia. To learn more about Robert Sardello, visit http://www.mythicjourneys.org/guest_sardello.html.

JAMIE L. MANSON, MDIV, received her degree from Yale Divinity School, where she studied Catholic theology and sexual ethics. Her column, "Grace on the Margins," appears weekly in the *National Catholic Reporter*. Her writing has won numerous awards, most recently second prize for 2012 Commentary of the Year from the Religion Newswriters Association. As a lay minister, she has worked extensively with New York City's poor and homeless populations. To learn more about Jamie Manson, visit http://jamiemanson.com/About_Me.html.

James D. Kirylo, PhD, is Associate Professor of Education at Southeastern Louisiana University. He has also taught at the University of South Alabama, Universidad Evángelica del Paraguay, and the University of Alabama at Birmingham. Among others, he has published works in the *Journal of Curriculum Theorizing, Journal of Curriculum and Pedagogy, Journal of Research on Christian Education*, and *Childhood Education*. His most recent book is *Paulo Freire: The Man from Recife*. James Kirylo can be reached at jkirylo@yahoo.com.

Cynthia Bourgeault, PhD, is a modern day mystic, Episcopal priest, writer, and internationally known retreat leader. Cynthia is the author of numerous books, including *The Meaning of Mary Magdalene, The Wisdom Jesus, Mystical Hope, The Wisdom Way of Knowing*, and *Love Is Stronger than Death*. The article in this edition of Oneing is adapted from her forthcoming book, *The Holy Trinity and the Law of Three*, which will be published by Shambhala Publications in July 2013. To learn more about Cynthia Bourgeault, visit http://www.contemplative.org/cynthia.html.

James Finley, PhD, lived as a monk at the cloistered Trappist monastery of the Abbey of Gethsemani in Kentucky, where the world-renowned monk and author, Thomas Merton, was his spiritual director. A clinical psychologist in private practice and a retreat and workshop leader, James Finley is the author of *Merton's Palace of Nowhere, The Contemplative Heart* and *Christian Meditation: Experiencing the Presence of God*. He will be presenting with Fr. Richard Rohr at the CAC-sponsored, April 2013 Conference, "Intimacy: The Divine Ambush." To learn more about James Finley, visit http://contemplativeway.org/.

INTRODUCTION

THE "PERENNIAL PHILOSOPHY" or "perennial tradition" is a term that has come in and out of popularity in Western and religious history, but has never been dismissed by the Universal Church. In many ways, it was actually affirmed at the Second Vatican Council, in their forward looking documents on ecumenism (*Unitatis Redintegratio*) and non-Christian religions (*Nostra Aetate*). It affirms that there are some constant themes, truths, and recurrences in all of the world religions.

In *Nostra Aetate*, for example, the Council Fathers begin by saying that "All peoples comprise a single community and have a single origin [created by one and the same Creator God].... And *one also is their final goal: God*.... The Catholic Church rejects nothing which is true and holy in these religions."[1] Then the document goes on to praise Native religion, Hinduism, Judaism, Buddhism, and Islam as "reflecting a ray of that truth which enlightens all people."[2] You have got to realize what courage and brilliance it took to write that in 1965, when very few people in any religion thought that way. In fact, most still don't think that way today.

One early exception was the great St. Augustine (354-430), a Doctor of the Church, who courageously wrote: "The very thing which is now called the Christian religion was not wanting among the ancients from the beginning of the human race until Christ came in the flesh. After that time, *the true religion, which had always existed, began to be called 'Christian.'*"[3] St. Clement of Alexandria, Origen, St. Basil, St. Gregory of Nyssa, and St. Leo the Great all held similar understandings before we got into the defensive (and offensive!)

modes of anti-Semitism and the Crusades. In some crucial ways, we have actually gone backward in religious history, when we should have been greasing the wheels of spiritual consciousness—forward.

The term is approximately used in the decree on priestly formation of the Council (*Optatam Totius*), where it states that seminarians should "base themselves on a philosophy which is perennially valid," and the decree encourages study of the entire history of philosophy and also "recent scientific progress."[4] They were probably thinking primarily of Scholastic philosophy; in truth, our term, as we use it here, is much more a theological statement than a philosophical one, anyway. This is Aldous Huxley's understanding, which is why he calls it a metaphysic, a psychology, and an ethic at the same time: "1) the metaphysic which recognizes a divine Reality substantial to the world of things and lives and minds; 2) the psychology that finds in the soul something similar to, or even identical to, divine Reality; 3) the ethic that places man's final end in the knowledge of the immanent and transcendent Ground of all being. This is immemorial and universal. Rudiments of the perennial philosophy may be found among the traditional lore of primitive peoples in every region of the world, and in its fully developed forms it has a place in every one of the higher religions."[5]

A Wisdom Tradition, as it can rightly be called, is what we hope to uncover and communicate in our literary and spiritual journal, which we are calling *Oneing*. The term is taken from my favorite Christian mystic, Lady Julian of Norwich (1342-1416), who used this old English term to describe what was happening between God and the soul. Although many translations of *Showings*, her major work, use words like "knitted," "enclosed" and "united" to make the same awesome point, we want to borrow this original word from her because the core message of our publication is that the divisions, dichotomies, and dualisms of the world can only be overcome by a *unitive consciousness* at every level: personal, relational, social, political, cultural, in inter-religious dialogue, and spirituality in particular. This is the unique and central job of healthy religion (re-ligio = to re-ligament!).

As Jesus put it in his great final prayer, "I pray that all may be one" (Jn 17:21). Or, as Julian put it, "By myself I am nothing at all, but in general, I AM in the oneing of love. For it is in this oneing that the life of all people exists."[6]

Many teachers have made the central, but oft-missed, point that *unity is not the same as uniformity*. Unity, in fact, is the reconciliation of differences, and those differences must be maintained—and yet overcome! You must actually distinguish things and separate them before you can spiritually unite them, usually at cost to yourself (Eph 2:14-16). If only we had made that simple clarification, so many problems—and overemphasized, separate identities—could have moved to a much higher level of love and service.

Paul already made this universal principle very clear in several of his letters. For example, "There is a variety of gifts, but it is always the same Spirit. There are all sorts of service to be done, but always to the same Lord, working in all sorts of different ways in different people. It is the same God working in all of them" (1 Cor 12:4-6). In his community at Ephesus, they were taught "There is one Lord, one faith, one baptism, one God who is Father of all, over all, through all, and within all, and each one of us has been given his own share of grace" (Eph 4:5-7).

We must finally go back to the ultimate Christian source for our principle—the central doctrine of the Trinity itself. Yes, God is "One," just as our Jewish ancestors taught us (Dt 6:4), and yet the further, more subtle, level is that this *oneness* is, in fact, the radical love union between *three* completely distinct "persons" of the Trinity. The basic principle and problem of "the one and the many" is overcome in God's very nature. God is a mystery of *relationship*, and the truest relationship is love. The three are not uniform—but quite distinct—and yet completely *oned* in total outpouring! Further, our word "person," now referring to an individual human being, was actually first used in Greek-based Trinitarian theology (*persona* = stage mask or a "sounding through"), and later then applied also to us! So we also are not autonomous beings, but soundings through, apart but radically one, too, just as Father, Son, and Holy Spirit are. The implications could make for years of meditation. We really are created in God's "image and likeness" (Gn 1:26f), much more than we ever imagined. Trinity is our universal template for the nature of reality and for how to "one"!

So we begin again at the CAC, after a wonderful first 25 years: many conferences, internships, and friendships, and our publication *Radical Grace*. We now enter into our next period of life, with an evolving vision and mission, symbolized by this new, more literary publication, and continuing to be led by our fine editor, Vanessa Guerin. In many ways, we hope this publication of the Rohr Institute can be the unique journal of our new Living School, which is also inaugurated this year. In all of these forums, we are not seeking some naïve "everything is one"; rather, we seek much more: the hard fought and much deeper "unity of the Spirit which was given us all to drink" (1 Cor 12:13). Here we must study, pray, wait, reconcile, and work to achieve true unity—not an impossible uniformity, which has been the tragic mistake of both an early notion of Christendom and a later notion of Communism.

We thank you for your trust, and may I both end and open this first issue of *Oneing* with another quote from dear Julian. She says, "The love of God creates in us such a *oneing* that when it is truly seen, no person can separate themselves from another person,"[7] and "In the sight of God all humans are oned, and one person is all people and all people are in one person."[8]

This is not some 21st century flabby fabrication. This is not pantheism or mere New Age optimism. This is the whole point; it was, indeed, supposed to usher in a new age—and it still will, and can. This is the perennial tradition. Our job is not to discover it, but only to retrieve what has been discovered—and enjoyed—again and again, in the mystics and saints of all religions.

As John the Beloved said, "I do not write to you because you do not know the truth, [we] are writing to you here because you know it already" (1 Jn 2:21).

Richard Rohr, OFM
January 6, 2013
Feast of the Epiphany/"Manifestation"

NOTES

1 *Nostra Aetate*, Vatican II, 1965, #1, 2.
2 Ibid.
3 Augustine of Hippo, *Retractiones*, 1:13.3, emphasis mine.
4 *Optatam Totius*, October 28, 1965, #15.
5 Aldous Huxley, *The Perennial Philosophy* (New York: Harper & Brothers, 1945), vii.
6 Julian of Norwich, *Showings*, 9.
7 Ibid., 65.
8 Ibid., 51.

I live my life in widening rings
which spread out to cover everything.
I may not complete the last one,
but I'll surely try:

I'm Circling around God, around the ancient tower,
and I've been circling for thousands of years —
and I don't yet know: am I a falcon, a storm,
or a vast song....

On the same evening, as again wind and clouds appeared.

Rainer Maria Rilke

Prayer [2] from *Prayers of a Young Poet: Rainer Maria Rilke*. Translated and
introduced by Mark S. Burrows © 2013 by Mark S. Burrows. Used by
permission of Paraclete Press. www.paracletepress.com.

Love at the Heart
of the Universe

By Ilia Delio, OSF, PhD

Gordon Moore, cofounder of Intel Corporation, predicted that the number of transistors on a chip would double approximately every two years, accelerating computing power and hence technological advancement. His prediction has been realized in the sense that technology now controls human culture in a breathless vortex of accelerating change. From wireless devices to artificial intelligence and robotics, technology has become the organizer of daily life. Beneath the surface of human change, however, there is a constancy shown in nature. Season after season the sun rises and sets; trees shed their leaves and give birth to new ones; animals die and new animals are born. To reflect on life through the window of nature is to see that change and constancy belong together. It is precisely because of constancy in nature that change is possible. What empowers this continuation of life despite periods of radical change?

COSMIC EVOLUTION

To look back over the history of the universe is to recognize a paradox of change and constancy. The ancient Greek philosophers, Heraclitus and Parmenides, disagreed precisely over this point. Heraclitus was a Stoic who held that change was the true stuff of reality, while Parmenides believed that change was illusory and that true reality is unchanging. The new universe story, however, provides some clues to this mystery of nature. Our Big Bang universe was born out of mystery, a quantum sea of energy that exploded into the fundamental forces of the universe. Space-time unfolded as the universe cooled and expanded; galaxies continue to move away from our own mid-size Milky Way galaxy, as our universe stretches into infinity. It took about 400 million years for the first stars to form and eons afterward for biological life to appear on this planet Earth. Time is the measurement of change, and the long periods of time required for new things to emerge in the cosmos means that change occurs slowly, sporadically, and is punctuated by long periods of stability and/or cataclysmic events. Up to the 19th century, biological nature was considered within the realm of fixed essences, whereby change came about through lawful mechanisms. However, the work of Charles Darwin and others showed that nature is marked by novelty. Nature does not simply rearrange the biological furniture, but gives rise to genuinely new entities. Changes in nature result from an interplay of law, chance, and deep time. The term "evolution" arose in the area of biology, although neither the term nor the idea of biological evolution began with Darwin. The Jesuit scientist Pierre Teilhard de Chardin described evolution as a movement toward complexified life forms during which, at critical points in the evolutionary process, qualitative differences emerge. The foundation of things is not so much a ground of being, sustaining its existence from beneath, as it is a power of attraction toward *what lies up ahead*. Evolution is not background to the human story; it is the human story.

In 1940 Teilhard completed his most important work, *The Human Phenomenon*, where he described the fourfold sequence of the evolution of galaxies, Earth, life, and consciousness. The human person is not a ready-made fact but the outflow of change—billions of years of evolution, beginning with cosmogenesis and the billions of years that led to biogenesis. The human person is integrally part of evolution in that we rise from the process but, in reflecting on the process, we stand apart from it. Teilhard said that *"we are nothing else than evolution become conscious of itself."*[1] We humans recapitulate the meaning and direction of the cosmos; evolution is a movement toward greater wholeness marked by a rise in consciousness.

Teilhard looked (albeit briefly) to the new science of quantum physics to understand the underlying energy of evolution. Quantum physics is based on the primacy of energy and the interconnectedness of all that exists. Reality is not a series of little elements but a flotsam of mass-energy. What quantum physics indicates is that, on the sub-atomic level, nothing exists in isolation; rather, everything exists as one interconnected whole, or what the physicist David Bohm called "implicate order." Being is intrinsically relational and exists as unbroken wholeness. Each part is connected with every other part. At the quantum level, autonomy is a misnomer. Rather, the whole is the basic reality. We are, fundamentally, wholes within wholes. Bohm wrote:

> The notion that all these fragments are separately existent is evidently an illusion, and this illusion cannot do other than lead to endless conflict and confusion. Indeed, the attempt to live according to the notion that the fragments are really separate is, in essence, what has led to the growing series of extremely urgent crises that is confronting us today. Thus, as is now well known, this way of life has brought about pollution, destruction of the balance of nature, over-population, world-wide economic and political disorder and the creation of an overall environment that is neither physically nor mentally healthy for most of the people who live in it. Individually there has developed a widespread feeling of helplessness and despair, in the face of what seems to be an overwhelming mass of disparate social forces, going beyond the control and even the comprehension of the human beings who are caught up in it.[2]

Surprisingly, the German philosopher Immanuel Kant recognized wholeness in nature long before modern science. An organized being is not a mere machine with only motive power, he indicated, but one with formative power. This formative power cannot be explained by the capacity of movement alone—that is, by mechanism —but by *something deep within nature itself.*[3]

Love is the faithful heart of the cosmos, the constancy of all life....

The properties of the parts are not intrinsic properties, but can be understood only within the context of the larger whole. What we call a part is merely a pattern in an inseparable web of relationships. Therefore the shift from parts to the whole can also be seen as a shift from objects to relationships. A system is an integrated whole whose essential properties arise from the relationships between its parts. Nature is an interlocking network of systems, an "unbearable wholeness of beings," as Steve Talbott wrote.[4] Nature is more flow than fixed, like a choreographed ballet or a symphony. Life evolves towards ever-increasing wholeness and consciousness, and something more—love.

WHAT'S LOVE GOT TO DO WITH IT?

TEILHARD SAID that the human experience of consciousness means that the stuff of the universe is mysteriously held together by something more than mere materiality. He speculated on two fundamental types of energy present in each individual element: a *tangential energy* making the element interdependent with all elements of the same order in the universe as itself, what we might call "bonding" energy, and a *radial energy* attracting the element in the direction of an ever more complex and centered state, which is "psychic" or conscious energy. The physical sciences observe the dissipation of energy and disintegration of matter, but they do not account for the continued growth, expansion and deepening of consciousness. The direction of evolution toward increased consciousness must be seen together with the evolution of integral wholeness. As life becomes more complex and conscious, it becomes more integrally whole. What accounts for evolution toward greater wholeness? Teilhard identified an energy of centration, whereby elements unite and complexify into greater wholeness, and called this "love-energy."

We are accustomed to thinking about love as a human sentiment or emotion, but Teilhard saw love as a passionate force at the heart of the Big Bang universe: the fire that breathes life into matter and unifies elements, center to center. "Love," he wrote, "is the *physical* structure of the universe."[5] It draws together and unites and, in uniting, it differentiates. Love is intrinsically relational, the affinity of being-with-being in a personal, centered way; a unity toward greater wholeness of being that marks all cosmic life. If there was no internal propensity to unite, even at a rudimentary level—indeed, in the molecule itself—Teilhard said, it would be physically impossible for love to appear higher up, in the human form. Love is the core of evolution.

GOD IN EVOLUTION

TO SEE THE universe through the eyes of love helps us make sense of evolution, not as a process of cold, blind chance or randomness, but one of passion, yearning, novelty, union, gift, suffering, death and new life. Love is the faithful heart of the cosmos, the constancy of all life; yet love seeks to become more being-in-love and hence is the energy of change. Nevertheless, this love is no mere physical energy. The name "God" points to this mystery of love in its unlimited depth, the center of all that is; love that overflows onto new life. God is not a super-natural Being hovering above earth, but the supra-personal whole, the Omega, who exists in all and through all. God *is* love—eternal, divine, overflowing, personal love. Love goes out to another for the sake of the other and manifests itself in relationship. Divine Love is personally relational—Trinity: Lover, Beloved and the Breath of Love. Divine Love, breathed forth into Word incarnate, marks the history of evolution, according to Teilhard. Every star, every galaxy, every leaf and bird breathed forth in Divine Love, reveals the Christ who is the personal unity of divine being-in-love. From all eternity God has sought to love another, to be love in another, and to be loved by the other forever—this other is the Christ who is the aim and purpose of this evolutionary universe.

Teilhard spent his life trying to show that evolution is not only the universe coming to be, but it is God who is *coming to be*. Divine Love, poured into space-time, rises in consciousness and erupts in the life of Jesus of Nazareth, becoming the pledge of our future in the risen Christ: "I am with you always until the end of the world" (Mt 28:20). We can read the history of our 13.7 billion year old universe as the rising up of Divine Love incarnate, which bursts forth in the person of Jesus, who reveals love's urge toward wholeness through reconciliation, mercy, peace and forgiveness. Jesus *is* the love of God incarnate, the wholemaker who shows the way of evolution toward unity in love. In Jesus, God breaks through and points us in a new direction; not one of chance or blindness but one of ever-deepening wholeness in love. In Jesus, God comes to us from the future to be our future. Those who follow Jesus are to become wholemakers, uniting what is scattered, creating a deeper unity in love.

FAITHFUL LOVE

CHRISTIAN LIFE IS a commitment to love, to give birth to God in one's own life and to become midwives of divinity in this evolving cosmos. We are to be wholemakers of love in a world of change. Teilhard saw that creativity and invention would forge the modern path of evolution, but he also saw that science alone cannot fulfill the cosmic longing for completion. God rises up at the heart of cosmic evolution through the power of love, which science and technology can facilitate but not surpass. The future of the earth, therefore, lies not in science and technology, but in the spiritual power of world religions and the power of love. We are born out of love, we exist in love and we are destined for eternal love. Instead of developing faster computers, smaller chips or artificial means of new life, it is time to reinvent ourselves in love. •

NOTES

1 Pierre Teilhard de Chardin, *The Human Phenomenon*, trans. Sarah Appleton-Weber (Brighton: Sussex Academic Press, 1999), 154.
2 David Bohm, *Wholeness and the Implicate Order* (New York: Routledge, 1995), 1-2.
3 Mark Taylor, *After God* (Chicago: University of Chicago Press, 2007), 315.
4 Stephen L. Talbott, "The Unbearable Wholeness of Beings," *The New Atlantis*, http://www.thenewatlantis.com/publications/the-unbearable-wholeness-of-beings.
5 Pierre Teilhard de Chardin, *Human Energy*, trans. J. M. Cohen (New York: Harcourt Brace Jovanovich, 1969), 72.

Ancient Wisdom for Contemporary Living

By David G. Benner, PhD

I HAVE ALWAYS BEEN drawn to the big-picture view of things. If some people climb mountains simply because they are there, I am always pulled toward summits by the promise of an ever-expanding vista. There is simply nothing like a macro perspective on life to help me live it on the micro level. This, to me, has always been the attraction of the Perennial Wisdom Tradition. To someone who is hardwired to seek a big-picture perspective on life, an encounter with perennial philosophy is like leading a child into a candy store!

However, because it is a stretch for most of us to think of philosophy as candy, let's talk about this tradition in terms that are more descriptive of what it truly is. Calling it the Perennial Wisdom Tradition draws our attention to the fact that it is a compilation of the deep sources of wisdom that have shaped human culture. Identifying the common core of the various wisdom traditions does not mean that the distinctives of the religious traditions it draws upon are unimportant. Christianity is not the same as Sufism, Islam the same as Baha'ism, or Taoism the same as Hinduism. The distinctives allow each separate tradition to speak with its own voice and tell its own story, but the common core allows us to hear that story in broader and deeper terms.

As a Christian, I find it encouraging that there is such a significant shared core to these various wisdom traditions. I find that it helps me understand my own tradition when I encounter it in the light of the spiritual wisdom that is quite easily found if one considers even the contours of the Perennial Wisdom Tradition. That is what I propose to do—simply look at the contours of this common core of wisdom. For even those, I think we will see, are enough to help us ground ourselves in, and align ourselves with, a reality that is vastly grander than what we usually realize.

CONTOURS OF THE PERENNIAL WISDOM TRADITION

ALL WISDOM TRADITIONS have something to say about four important matters: the nature of ultimate reality, the possibilities for human knowing of this ultimate reality, the nature of personhood, and the goal of human existence. In what follows, I will draw together some of the central insights of the world's wisdom traditions associated with each of these four areas and conclude with several important consequences for living that flow from these observations. I do so as a psychologist interested in spirituality, not as someone with expertise in philosophy, religion or theology. Fortunately, that's the whole point of the Perennial Wisdom Tradition—it offers ancient wisdom for contemporary living that is relevant to all of us, not just to a few.

ULTIMATE REALITY

HOWEVER NAMED, GOD is the Ultimate Reality. Language does not serve well to describe this Ultimate Reality since it is so profoundly supra-human and trans-personal. Yet, humans need to name things in order to communicate and so, across time and the various wisdom traditions, we have adopted such linguistic handles as Spirit, Divine Presence, The Wholly Other, The One, or The Ground of Being. All names for this foundation of existence point to the same reality—a reality that, at the same time, is both transcendent and immanent, not set apart from the world of humans and things but deeply connected to everything that is.

All names fail miserably in the task of capturing Ultimate Reality. How easily we forget that language does not hold reality; at its best, it merely points toward it. Our problem, however, is that we confuse our puny constructs and construals with the reality to which they, even at their best, only point.

Anthony de Mello tells a very short story from the Perennial Wisdom Tradition that nicely illustrates this.

> The master encouraged his followers to look at the moon by pointing toward it but noticed that his followers inevitably looked at his finger, not the moon.[1]

The story tells us that Ultimate Reality will always lie beyond all the fingers, those images and concepts that we use to point toward it. We must, therefore, be ever vigilant in realizing the danger of getting stuck in our words and concepts rather than getting in touch with the reality behind them. This is true in all of life, but nowhere more true than when we use words to attempt to point toward the Wholly Other that is Ultimate Reality.

Ultimate Reality is the source, substance and sustenance of all that is. Nothing exists without it. To be removed from this vital connection would be to instantly cease to exist. We exist because we are in relation to Ultimate Reality or, more precisely, because we exist within it.

THE POSSIBILITY OF ULTIMATE KNOWING

THIS RAISES, HOWEVER, a crucial question. If this assertion about the nature of Ultimate Reality is to have any meaning for us, it must be knowable in some way. The mystics of the Perennial Wisdom Tradition assert that direct, immediate knowing is possible. They tell us that such knowing is not based on reason

We come from a tradition of both faith and reason.

or deduction, but on communion. We only truly know that with which we become one. Communion is a knowing through union. Knowledge of God, then, means union with God—something that the mystics have always proclaimed to be not just possible, but the goal and fulfilment of humanity.

Knowing is, therefore, becoming one with that which we seek to know. We see this in the Hebrew Bible's use of the language of knowing to describe sexual intercourse (as in "Adam knew Eve"). Knowing is intimate, and this intimacy is transformational. We come to resemble that which we know. The more we resemble that which we seek to know, the more we truly know it, and the more truly we know it, the more we are one with it.

Union is not sameness but likeness. However, in union, the dualism that initially separates subsequently dissolves, and we experience the unity that holds us both. This is, of course, a profound mystery—a mystery that lies beyond understanding but not beyond experiential knowing.

THE MYSTERY OF PERSONHOOD

THE POSSIBILITY OF human knowing of Ultimate Reality also lies in the fact that humans are a reflection of this reality that is remarkably similar to its source. All personal knowing is based in likeness. We can only truly know that which we already resemble in some important way. This possibility lies in the human soul, where we retain traces of our origin. In other words, the ground of our being is the Ground of Being.

This brings us right to the core of the mystery of human personhood. Humans are especially connected to Ultimate Reality because, in some mysterious way, the human soul contains something similar to, possibly even identical with, the Ultimate Reality we name as God. Humans are a unique expression of this reality. The depths of the human soul mirror the depths of Spirit. There is a place in the depths of our soul in which Ultimate Reality alone can dwell, and within which we dwell in Ultimate Reality. Meister Eckhart says that the nameless depth in me cries out to the nameless depth in God—our profound human mystery crying out to the divine mystery, beyond names, forms and distinctions, that is our source and ground.

To be—as described in the Christian tradition—made in the image of Ultimate Mystery, means that humans will inevitably be a fundamental mystery to themselves. Human mystery is an echo of Ultimate Reality. The key to knowing human mystery is knowing Ultimate Reality, and the key to knowing the mystery of Ultimate Reality is meeting that Reality in the depths of the human soul.

THE GOAL OF HUMAN EXISTENCE

THE KNOWING THAT humans seek, in every cell of our being, is to know the source and ground of our existence. This, the Perennial Wisdom Tradition teaches, is the goal and meaning of being human. Life has a direction. All of life flows from and returns to Divine Presence. Our Origin is our Destiny! So, as the river said to the seeker, "Do I really have to fret about the journey? No matter which way I turn, I'm homeward bound!"

Once again, words do a very poor job of describing this direction of the flow of human life. In the Christian tradition we speak of union with the Divine—sometimes daring to adopt the even bolder language of *theosis,* or divinization. Take, for example, the words spoken by the priest when mixing the water and the wine in the Roman Catholic Mass—"By the mystery of this water and wine may we come to share in the divinity of Christ who humbled himself to share in our humanity." Union with Ultimate Reality is sharing the divinity of Christ. It is participating in the Divine Presence. This is the fulfillment of humanity.

CONSEQUENCES FOR LIVING

I MPORTANT IMPLICATIONS for living flow from the appreciation of the fact that the purpose of life is this unitive knowing of the ground of our being. When identified solely with our bodies, minds, experiences or other lesser things, we lack full awareness of our spiritual nature and the truth of the ground of our being. The moral of the Perennial Wisdom Tradition is, "Don't settle for anything less than the truth of your Christ-self." The ego-self, with which we are all much more familiar, is a small cramped place when compared with the spaciousness of our true self-in-Christ. This is the self that is not only at one within itself; it is at one with the world, and with all others who share it as their world. It is, therefore, one with Ultimate Reality.

Life, therefore, is a constant flow of invitations to awaken to these spiritual realities. Spiritual practices are, at their best, cooperation with life's inherent tendency toward spiritual awakening and unfolding—a tendency that Christians name as grace. Awakening is the expression of that grace in which we see through our apparent separation and notice that we are already one with Divine Presence and with all that is. All that is missing is awareness. •

NOTES

1 William Dych, SJ, *Anthony de Mello: Writings* (Maryknoll, NY: Orbis Books, 2008), 15.

The Perennial
Tradition in an Age
of Globalization

By John L. Esposito, PhD

A S I THINK ABOUT the widespread reemergence of the
Perennial Tradition, I realize that my own life experiences
reflect the changing conditions that led us, in the 20th
century, to other world religions: to an appreciation for their insights
and then, even in the midst of their diversity, to the discovery of how
congruent their visions of deep truths are with each other.

Raised an Italian-American Roman Catholic in "the one true
church," I studied with the Capuchin Franciscan Fathers in New
York, Massachusetts and New Hampshire, for ten years (from age 14
to 24). I left two years before ordination, but my interest in religion
continued. After earning a Master of Arts in Catholic Theology
at St. John's University, I taught theology and Bible (1966-72) at

a Catholic women's college, Rosemont College in Pennsylvania. I then decided to study at Temple University in Philadelphia, where I could earn a PhD in Catholic thought at a secular university.

Temple's Religion Department, a World Religions Department rather than the more common Theology or Religious Studies Department, was distinctive. Temple's faculty had to be born into, or be converts to, the religious tradition that they taught; course offerings focused on all the world's major religions and PhD students were required to major in one religion and minor in two others. For me, studying world religions (Hinduism, Buddhism, Chinese and Japanese religions) was amazingly transformative. Never looking back, I switched my focus from Catholicism to Hinduism and Zen Buddhism. Encouraged by my professor to write a dissertation in Hindu studies, I went to see Bernard Phillips, the founding Chair of the Department, to discuss my intended research, but Phillips suggested that I study Islam! I was astonished and dismayed. Why would I want to learn about *that* religion?

Raised in Brooklyn, where everyone seemed to be Italian, Irish or Jewish, I knew about the 1967 Arab-Israeli war through reports from the American press. I had also been deeply moved by the movie, *The Exodus*, which at that time I thought was historically accurate. I could not imagine why anyone would want to deal with Arabs or study Islam. While my initial response to Professor Phillips was a polite but resolute "No, thank you!" here I am, thirty years later, having devoted an entire career to the study of Islam and Muslim societies! The reaction of friends and family to my decision to study Islam was unanimously negative. A fellow graduate student, who specialized in Roman Catholic thought, exclaimed "Why go into that 'abracadabra' field? You'll never get a job." So, what attracted me? How could a "No" become a lifelong profession, or even a vocation?

Finally acquiescing to Professor Phillips' forceful suggestion, I took the Islam course, and was astonished to discover another Abrahamic faith. Could there actually be a Judeo-Christian-Islamic tradition? If Muslims recognized many of the major patriarchs and prophets of Judaism and Christianity, as well as God's revealed books—the Torah and the Message (New Testament) of Jesus—why had I not been aware of this after all my years of liberal arts and theological training? Islam did not consider itself to be a new religion, but rather as communicating a final revelation, incorporating the perennial wisdom of the past. The Quran describes Abraham, Moses, Jesus, Mary and others as "Muslim" (meaning that they had submitted to God's will). Sufism, the mystical tradition of Islam, emphasizes the concept of a single religious truth.

Temple's unique program proved prescient. The religious landscape was dramatically changing. Religion in America in the mid-20th century had been well described by Will Herberg's 1955 pioneering study, *Protestant, Catholic and Jew: an Essay in American Religious Sociology*. However, by 1965 a sea-change began to occur, with the impact of the reforms of Vatican II (1962-65), calls for the secularization of Christian doctrine and theology, and the growing presence and interest in Eastern religions and spirituality.

In 1965, Harvey Cox published *The Secular City*, a stunningly popular book that sold more than one million copies. At the time, Cox, whose later books continue to reflect insightful predictions of change amidst the dynamic religious scene, maintained that the impact of secularization had resulted in "man turning his attention away from worlds beyond and toward this world and this time."[1] The new "technopolis," said Cox, had no use for either religion or an afterlife, and therefore the task of the modern theologian was to learn to "speak of God in a secular fashion." At the same time, a group of reformist—sometimes seen as radical—European and American "Death of God" theologians addressed similar issues. Christian theologians like Gabriel Vahanian, Paul van Buren, and William Hamilton argued that modern secular culture had lost all sense of the sacred, and that the concept of transcendence had lost any meaningful place in modern thought. They concluded that, for the modern mind, "God is dead," and advocated a post-Christian theology in which Jesus, as the Christ of faith, was the model or ideal human whose example of love and compassion was to be emulated in a church community. Clearly, this trend strongly challenged traditional Western religious thought, and led many to search elsewhere for "the truth."

Cox's Secular City would soon be overtaken by a seeming *invasion* of Eastern spiritual masters and teachings, a phenomenon that Cox would chronicle in 1977 in *Turning East: the Promise and Peril of the New Orientalism*. "Eastern Religions" fast became part of America's religious landscape. Universities and colleges, whose curriculum had been dominated predominantly by Christianity and Judaism, now expanded their offerings, hiring specialists in non-Western religions, in particular Hinduism and Buddhism, and then eventually in Islam. Disaffected Christians and Jews turned to Eastern gurus, yogis, mystics and Zen masters, and sought out meditation-based spiritual paths.

These trends were reflected in popular courses I offered on world religions and comparative mysticism at the College of the Holy Cross. Students in my course on Mystics and Zen Masters accompanied me on unique and, for some, religiously worrisome, field trips to St. Joseph's Abbey in Spencer, Massachusetts and the Insight Meditation Society in Barre, Massachusetts—now a major Buddhist center—in order to learn more about, and briefly experience, Christian and Buddhist forms of meditation. The Trappists of Spencer were especially interesting because, under their Abbot Thomas Keating, they had pioneered Centering Prayer and Christian-Buddhist meditation, joining in particular with the great Japanese Zen Master, Joshu Sasaki Roshi, at the Abbey.

My study and teaching of both world religions and comparative mysticism revealed not only the distinctive religious differences but also commonalities, especially in the meaning behind religious discourse and practices. Nowhere did this deeper meaning surface more than in the writings of experts, spiritual masters and texts, past and present: those of the Christian saints (John of the Cross, Theresa of Avila, Julian of Norwich) and the anonymous author of the Cloud of Unknowing, as well as the Hindu Shankara, the Buddhist Nagarjuna, and Muslim mystics like Ibn Arabi, Mansur al-Hallaj and Jalaluddin Rumi, described as the "most popular poet in America." My new awareness was also fostered by more recent scholars and teachers of mysticism like Thomas Merton, Bede Griffiths, David Steindl-Rast and a host of Hindus and Buddhists (Joseph Goldstein, Sharon Salzberg, Sri Dharma Pravartaka Acharya, Ram Dass, Sri Chinmoy) and Muslims like Seyyed Hossein Nasr, Bawa Muhaiyaddeen, and Annemarie Schimmel.

During this time, all of my past experiences and study seemed to converge as I learned more about the modern-day Islamically-rooted Traditionalist school of thought within Sufism (Islamic mysticism). Like all the wisdom schools, it offers spiritual paths that return to their source, that can co-exist with, but also transcend, institutional religion. Also, like all the wisdom schools,

...the great world religious traditions share the same deep truths from which all belief systems have developed.

it places primacy on religion as a spiritual path, a life rooted in contemplation, a worldview that appreciates both the unity and diversity of religions, and thus embraces a religious pluralism that is essential, in an age of globalization and in our multi-religious and multi-ethnic societies.

The scholar-practitioners who belong to the Primordial Tradition or Wisdom School included Huston Smith (a philosopher at MIT and author of *The Forgotten Tradition*) and Seyyed Hossein Nasr (an Islamic scholar at George Washington University and author of *Living Sufism* and *Sufi Essays*), as well as German-Swiss philosopher Frithjof Schuon (author of *The Transcendent Unity of Religions*) and Martin Lings (a British scholar and author of *A Sufi Saint of the Twentieth Century*). These were all part of the broader movement, often referred to as the Perennial Philosophy or Perennialism, whose understandings were well described by Huston Smith, Aldous Huxley and Gottfried Leibniz. Smith captured the essence of their belief: "If we take the world's enduring religions at their best, we discover the distilled wisdom of the human race."

However different, all advocate the rediscovery of the wisdom traditions of the past, believing that the various visions of the great world religious traditions share the same deep truths from which all belief systems have developed. They distinguish between two interconnected planes of reality and knowing, scientific empiricism and a transcendent/immanent reality, experienced in wisdom traditions through meditation and contemplation. Religious language or discourse, theology, laws, symbols, and rituals of institutional religion, conditioned by historical, social and cultural contexts, are seen as means, as metaphors and "pointers," to the divine, not as ends in themselves.

However diverse religious traditions appear, these wisdom schools affirm a belief in the transcendent Unity of all religions and, as perennial philosophy maintains, there is a divine reality that enables universal truth to be understood.

While there is an underlying unity, there is also a diversity of conceptualizations of the ultimate reality, and multiple interpretations. Thus, the ultimate reality is described as at once transcendent and immanent, personal and impersonal; it is identified by diverse names (God, Yahweh, Allah, Vishnu, Shiva, Nirvana or Buddhahood) and is often experienced differently. Each religion is a unique way to know divine reality and to reach spiritual enlightenment or salvation.

For those of us living in the 21st century—an age of globalization, mass migrations, and increasingly multi-religious and multi-ethnic societies—mutual understanding and respect, based on religious pluralism rather than religious exclusivism, are extremely critical to our survival. The insights from the perennial tradition have much to contribute in developing and strengthening multi-faith relations. Its insights help to combat religious discrimination and conflicts between and within religious traditions, and to develop more pluralistic paths of religious spirituality. Today, in the 21st century, we see scholars and spiritual teachers forging new, more inclusive spiritual paths that recognize other religious traditions as sources of insight and wisdom. They are informed by the teachings and spiritual practices (meditation and contemplation) of multiple religious traditions. As Richard Rohr emphasizes, "If it is true, then it has to be true everywhere." •

NOTES

1 Harvey Cox, *The Secular City: Secularization and Urbanization in Theological Perspective* (New York: The Macmillan Company, 1965), 1-2.

A Hopeful Discontent

Tracing Authentic Spirituality Through Christian History

The Rohr Institute's Joelle Chase interviews Diana Butler Bass, PhD, Christian historian and author of numerous books, including Christianity After Religion: The End of Church and the Birth of a New Spiritual Awakening *and* A People's History of Christianity: The Other Side of the Story.

JOELLE CHASE: In this issue of *Oneing*, the Perennial Tradition, we are exploring the truth that continuously recurs within the world's sacred paths, pointing to Divine Reality in all things and the goal of existence as union with that reality. From your own background—now as an Episcopalian, previously as an Evangelical—and as a historian who studies Christianity, how would you define tradition?

DIANA BUTLER BASS: Much of my work centers around ideas of tradition, what tradition is and what tradition isn't. I often refer to a definition of tradition that was developed by the great 20th-century church historian, Jaroslav Pelikan, a Lutheran who eventually converted to Orthodoxy. Pelikan said that tradition is the living faith of the dead, and traditionalism is the dead faith of the living.

I love this, because I think the essence of Divine Reality means we're all connected, and it makes sense to think about tradition as this living thing we inherit from people who have gone on before us—their experiences; the poetry, words, art and beauty that matter to them; the insights that they learned from their own lives.

It becomes problematic when we freeze-frame the things they've passed on to us, and we act as if tradition wasn't a lived experience, but instead some sort of unchangeable, antiquated vase that we don't like. Then tradition passes over to traditionalism. Many people think they're adhering to tradition when actually they have just become traditionalists. Instead of living it, they have ritualized the experience of their predecessors, losing the essential connection with spirit that animated the original experience. For the last decade I have been thinking, writing, and talking much about living and experiencing tradition, and how we connect with our ancient faith, letting it sing in our own lives.

JOELLE: You've said in your book, *A People's History of Christianity*, that tradition is important to keeping the faith strong and alive and whole; that there is danger in losing our roots, the history of our faith. And yet, as you just shared, we don't want to freeze-frame our faith or let it become stagnant. How can we find the balance to claim and embrace our tradition while being inclusive, open, and fluid?

DIANA: Only recently has our culture begun to welcome, with the rise of post-modernism, a connection with our past. During the 17th through early 19th centuries there was a large-scale philosophical rejection of tradition in favor of whatever was modern or innovative, but now we have a new opportunity to claim our past. For me this raises the question, "What part of the past do you claim?"

Does the tradition include, say, Hildegard of Bingen? For many years the tradition didn't include Hildegard. She was too controversial. People had forgotten about her. There wasn't a place for a woman who was a doctor and a theologian and a lay preacher, so the church let the memory of Hildegard of Bingen lay waste. It's only been in the last 30 or 40 years, as we've gone back into history and asked the question again — "What counts?" — that she's been recovered.

Tradition is much more flexible than we often think it is, and whenever we talk about tradition it inevitably involves conflict — whose tradition matters and who gets to say which tradition matters. I like to call this a lively argument for the entire history of the church, and the church is richer for it! The post-modern movement has opened our eyes to that broadness of the past and how we might re-appropriate it.

JOELLE: What counts for you when you're looking back through the church's past and claiming pieces for yourself?

DIANA: That's the big question! When I wrote the book *A People's History of Christianity* that was one of the things I had to try to figure out. What would really count as a history that people who read my book would find meaningful? In the 21st century, people are not very interested in the history of institutions — of denominations and organized church, popes and buildings and theologians and "great men" — which has been the primary focus of Christian history. Those things are beautiful and they're part of that big wide swath of Christian experience, but we have generally *only* told those stories.

So I ask myself where people's interests are now, where do we find God, how do we connect with God? I think we often find God in each other, so I search history for simple people, people like me, who loved God. I make friends with the most common people and find God in their stories.

JOELLE: In your book *A People's History of Christianity*, you juxtapose the Great Commandment — to love your neighbor as yourself and to love God — and the Great Commission — the words attributed to Jesus, "Go and make disciples of all nations." You say these two commands affect our perspective in dramatically different ways. Would you talk about how these "Greats" influence history and our own lived spirituality?

DIANA: I think it's fascinating that Protestants in particular love the Great Commission. Historical-critical scholars over the last century have studied this passage at the end of the Gospel of Matthew in depth and, I think, rather successfully shown that it was a later addition to the gospel. "Go and baptize all nations" are probably not words that Jesus spoke, but were added quite a bit later. Yet here we have whole traditions that have taken those words and made them the central point of the gospel—to evangelize the whole earth.

The contra-command—the command to love God and to love your neighbor as yourself—scholars believe Jesus actually said. So those words, as far as we are aware, are completely genuine to Jesus' teaching, and are at its center. "Love God and love your neighbor as yourself" is really the theological turning point of all four gospels, and certainly the letters of Paul. This framework of love should be at the middle of all of our understanding of what the church is and what evangelism is; the point from which everything else spins out.

Of all the things that we need

in the 21st century,

If you have a Great Commission without the Great Command, if you just go out and evangelize people and you aren't paying attention to loving God and loving neighbor as yourself, you are always going to wind up in a bad place. The Great Commission without the Great Command is intolerance, militarism and crusades. The Great Command, to love God and love your neighbor, without the Great Commission, on the other hand, can wind up being kind of self-centered, but at least it's a loving isolated reality.

What if we take the command to love, and we understand it as our commission? What does that look like? The doing of social justice, serving the poor, really listening to and being friends with people in other religions. That's what I dream for the 21st century—a church that can re-center itself in love and yet, not simply say, "we feel loving and that's good enough," but to take that love and to reinterpret the Great Commission, not as a triumphal spread of Christianity, but as the humble spread of God's dream for justice and harmony here and now.

JOELLE: You've mentioned Hildegard of Bingen, who had some beautiful ideas and images on cosmic unity. We can follow the thread of unity throughout Christian history, though it seems to be emerging even more strongly today. How do you see the truth of union—Divine Reality undergirding all things—fitting into Christian tradition and faith?

DIANA: When I think of Hildegard, I think of circles, mandalas, a symphony, people dancing or moving together in a fluid way. For Hildegard, connection was organic, not about straight lines. When I think about this through the lens of mainstream Christian tradition, I tend to think about the cross, two lines perpendicular to one another. We have emphasized the cross as the central symbol of Christianity and not the circle, which has created an unbalanced understanding of the story. I think Jesus and his followers spent

I think imagination

is at the top of the list.

more time in circles—sitting around a campfire or dancing at a wedding—during their time together, when they were journeying through ancient Israel, than they actually spent contemplating this instrument of torture, the cross.

I love the Celtic cross because it combines the lines and the angularity of the Christian cross with the circle, reminding us that an organic unity is central to Christianity, and somehow it's both of those things. I like thinking about alternative symbols for Christianity; we can get so stuck on the two or three expected images, stories, or interpretations, that our imagining of what it means to be a person living in and through God is limited. Anything that challenges the narrow vision of Christian tradition is a benefit for my spiritual life and, I think, for the life of the church. Of all the things that we need in the 21st century, I think imagination is at the top of the list.

JOELLE: You seem hopeful for Christianity's future. Could you give a few examples of things that make you most hopeful, that indicate the Christian faith is headed toward more love, more union?

DIANA: This will probably sound strange, but one of the things that I find most hopeful right now is that so many people are angry at the church. Catholics are angry at the Catholic Church; Protestants are angry at all different kinds of Protestant churches. I have Orthodox and fundamentalist friends who are angry at their churches. I know more people who are angry at their churches than I know who are happy with their churches. You can think of it as a terrible thing and that we should despair, but it really is a sign of hope.

If people were content with business-as-usual church, what kind of hope would that be? It would just mean that people were happy with a kind of conventional, religious pablum. Many churches are not offering a robust vision of what it really means to live a radical life of the beauty of God through Jesus Christ. People are discontented with churches that are just offering them the same old answers or the same old liturgy. To me, that's the greatest sense of hope there can possibly be, because people are hungry for more.

Being angry at the church, throughout the whole history of Christianity in the last 2,000 years, has always been the seed bed of spiritual renewal, reformation or new movements. St. Augustine said, "Hope has two beautiful daughters: Anger and Courage. Anger at the way things are. Courage to ensure they don't stay that way." So if discontent is the beginning, hey, we must be at the beginning of something amazing. Everybody's angry. That's my greatest sense of hope.

JOELLE: What do you think that "something amazing" is going to be?

DIANA: I think it has something to do with this combining of things that we've been talking about, that somehow it's going to be a reinterpretation of the whole tradition on the basis of "love God and love your neighbor." I think there will be a combining of the circles of Hildegard of Bingen with the angularity of the traditional symbol of the cross. And it will come from listening to the voices on the fringes, helping us reinterpret and re-imagine our faith. •

A Franciscan Spirituality of Love, Beauty and Moral Living

By Mary Beth Ingham, CSJ, PhD

For John Duns Scotus and, indeed, for the Franciscan tradition, no moral journey can be taken without reference to a relationship with God. Indeed, Scotus grounds the entirety of moral living on the single precept, "God is to be loved." Here is a moral vision framed in love, guided by love and achieved in love. It begins with desire and ends in a friendship that extends to all persons and all beings. Moral living is grounded in a spirituality of love and fed by the experience of beauty. Let us explore the contours of this journey of love as Scotus explains it to us.

Moral living is grounded in a spirituality of love and fed by the experience of beauty.

Moral living is, at heart, relational living. The relationship that Scotus highlights is that of the Covenant. The Covenant, given by God to Moses and to the People of Israel, is comprised of two basic commandments: love God and love one another. For Scotus, the commands of the second tablet of the Ten Commandments (those that relate to the neighbor) are in harmony (*consona*) with the first command, to love God above all things. This means, quite simply, that our love for our neighbor is the expression of our love for God, for how can we love the God we do not see if we fail to love the neighbor whom we do see (1 Jn 4:20)? What's more, our moral living expresses a deep harmony with our spirituality and incarnates our relationship of love for God.

Scotus explains that a simple meditation upon love can help us see why it is not simply the heart of moral living but is, in fact, the *objective* ground for all we do. When we reflect upon the first commandment more carefully, we recognize that the command, to love God above all, actually further specifies the first practical principle, "God is to be loved." If God is the highest and most beautiful good, then God should be loved beyond all other goods, and for God alone. The theological virtue of charity captures our love for God. Since we are naturally drawn to love the good, we are naturally drawn to love God. Charity, the theological virtue of love for God, focuses and intensifies our natural desires and inclinations to love and seek the good. Charity is that virtue which inclines me to love the good in the person of God as highest good.

This is not all, however. In loving God, I discover a three-fold dimension to the *objectivity* of loving. The three-fold dimension leads me from my own desires to the experience of loving friendship. Scotus explains the gradual deepening of my experience of love as *objective* grounding by means of a guided meditation that has three distinct stages. First, think about *objective* in terms of that "object" which is suited by nature, in itself, to satisfy the desire to love. Such an object would be the true end or goal of all loving. Understood in this way, this term *objective* certainly refers to the good, as the object of all desire. This term applies to God in this fullest sense, since God alone is the most perfect, most beautiful being, suited by nature to satisfy the longings of the human heart.

God is the object of love in this fullest sense. Indeed, since God is the highest good, God is the only necessary object of love. This makes the command to love God ("God is to be loved") the only necessary command of the moral law. It is the most perfect human act of which we are capable. Scotus explains this insight in the following way:

> For something must be loved most of all, and it is none other than the highest good, even as this good is recognized by the intellect as that to which we must adhere most.[1]

There is a second way that we can understand the objectivity of love. *Objective* can also refer to the precise aspect according to which a person or thing is loved. In this way, God is loved according to the degree that the divine nature is self-revealing and perceived as a good by anyone who seeks the highest good. This second meaning moves beyond the first as personal moves beyond impersonal. In the first sense of *objective*, "highest good" and "divine being" can be identified as the most appropriate object of my love. Yet these terms do not necessarily have any personal qualities, nor is it necessary that the highest good love me in return. There is no greater sadness than unrequited love!

What is specific about this second meaning of *objective* is that it implies what is most important in the Judeo-Christian understanding of God, i.e., the act of self-revelation (Ex 3:14) and divine initiative (Jn 3:16). In the act of divine self-revelation, God has established the possibility for reciprocity or mutuality with us. This free desire on the part of God established the relationship in the Covenant. The Covenant is a pact that gives further basis to the moral law ("love your neighbor") as *precise* expression of how God wills that we treat one another. God did not only establish the Covenant; God chose to become incarnate, to be Emmanuel, God-with-us. Such an act of love inspires our gratitude and reveals the motivation behind our obedience: "If you love me, keep my commandments" (Jn 15:9-17).

These two meanings of *objective* reveal the dynamic nature of charity. I begin to love God because I recognize that God is infinite goodness and, therefore, the most appropriate object of love. However, my initial love for God is returned and intensified through communion with the divine Trinity of persons which I discover as the direct result, not of my loving, but of God's initiative toward me. I am invited into a communion of loving friendship. This relationship of friendship continues to increase in its dynamism and intensifies my own acts of love. In addition, the dynamic extends to others, once I recognize that God is not "my good" or my personal possession, but everyone's good.

At this point, neither God nor moral actions are the focus of impersonal or legalistic reflection. Now the personal, spiritual relationship of love informs all our actions and moral choices. Now we begin to see the creation of co-lovers, members of a moral community.

Scotus explains how this increasing dynamic of love and friendship continues to grow to include God's gifts to us: creation, the Incarnation, and the promise of eternal reward. Our love for God feeds on God's love for us.

> For just as in our case someone is first loved honestly, that is, primarily because of himself or herself, and only secondarily because such a one returns our love, so that this reciprocal love in such a person is a special reason of amiability over and above the objective goodness such a person possesses, so too in God. Not only does God's infinite goodness, or his nature as this unique nature in its uniqueness, draw us to love such, but because this "Goodness" loves me, sharing itself with me, therefore I elicit an act of love towards it. And under this second aspect of amiability, one can include everything about God that proves his love for us, whether it be creation or redemption or preparing us for beatitude in heaven...hence he deserves to be loved in return, according to that text from John: "Let us love God because he has first loved us."[2]

This second meaning of *objective* refers to a reciprocal or mutual relationship common to friendship. Such a personal relationship is *objective* in the sense that it "transcends the subject" or functions as "inter-subjectivity."

...God is loved as that good which makes the lover completely happy.

What's more, this second dimension points to the need for revelation, since where else do we find a record of the history of God's initiative toward us? While the first meaning of *objective* was possible to natural reasoning alone, the second meaning is only possible when we recognize that God is a Trinity of persons who has taken initiative in human history. Human history is truly salvation history. In scripture we discover a God who remains faithful, despite our infidelity. Now the focus of our reflection has shifted from our love for God to God's love for us.

The third and final meaning of *objectivity* refers to the consequences of the activity of loving: the satisfaction and delight which accompanies the activity of loving God. This third meaning refers to the satisfying happiness and joy God gives as our ultimate end. Inasmuch as this satisfaction inevitably accompanies this act of love, it serves as a kind of object, for why would we want to deny ourselves such exquisite delight? In this last sense God is loved as that good which makes the lover completely happy. And here, our love of God is the highest (most complete) of all. We love God as our delight, and under that aspect of God that is most delightful to us: as our faithful friend. Scotus states this insight very simply:

> The third meaning [of *objective*] refers to the satisfying happiness God gives as our ultimate end, although this is not properly speaking a formal objective reason, since it is a natural consequence of the elicited act of loving him. Nevertheless, inasmuch as this satiety inevitably accompanies this act of love, it could serve as a kind of object. And in this sense God is loved inasmuch as he is that good object that makes us completely happy and he is said to be loved in this way insofar as

he is loved supremely, that is, not *qua* formal object, but under an aspect in the object that accompanies the act of loving it.[3]

Although Scotus does not use the term here, we could understand this as a reference to divine beauty, especially in light of the example that this Franciscan provides to illustrate what he has been talking about.

As any good teacher might, Scotus concludes this discussion with an example that illustrates all three aspects of *objectivity*. It is an example of beauty, and he refers us to an experience of a beautiful object. Suppose, Scotus suggests, that there is in nature something which exceeds all other things in beauty. It is the highest possible and most beautiful being. Now, suppose as well that this most beautiful being were also the source of the eye's ability to see it and, in addition, suppose that the activity of vision itself delighted in this sight. Then, he concludes, in seeing this object, the eye's love of seeing would be satisfied to the full.

Such a reflection on the experience of beauty reveals what grounds all reality, and what sustains the journey taken by the human heart. The primary reason for charity, and the purest motivation of our love for God, is found in the divine nature as worthy of love. The other two reasons why we love God refer more to the activity of loving, both in terms of personal delight and the good of relationship. However, we need charity; we need the theological virtue of love in order for us to sustain our relationship with God.

There are two reasons for this. First, in this life, we are unable to focus our attention adequately on what we love. We cannot recollect all our faculties, so that we might exert the effort we would if our powers were united and all impediments removed. Here charity aids us in loving God "with our whole heart, mind, soul and strength." Secondly, human loving does not possess the intensity required for such loving. A key theological virtue, charity, adds a further intensity and focus to what is already present in our act of love. This adds what we ourselves could do if we exerted a bit more effort. But charity helps us and makes it easier for us to do more with a bit less effort. In this way, charity is not *supernatural*, in the sense that it provides us with an intensity we could not achieve on our own. Rather, charity is a theological virtue insofar as it focuses our act of love more carefully upon God as highest object of love.

Scotus offers us an ethics of divine relationship. The journey begins with our natural inclination to love the good, and the highest good beyond all else. Charity helps to complete the journey as we enter into a reciprocal relationship of friendship with God and, ultimately, with the Trinity.

While it may be true that the moral law is ultimately founded on God's will, as revealed in the Ten Commandments, the divine will belongs to a Trinitarian mystery of love, communion and mutual self-gift. For the Franciscan tradition, the choice to live a moral life is, quite simply, a choice to enter into a relationship, a Covenant, with God, and with all persons as children of God. •

NOTES

1 John Duns Scotus, *Ordinatio*, III, d. 27.
2 Ibid.
3 Ibid.

What's So Perennial About the Perennial Philosophy?

By James P. Danaher, PhD

> *Every individual is at once the beneficiary and the victim of the linguistic tradition into which he has been born—the beneficiary inasmuch as language gives access to the accumulated records of other people's experience, the victim insofar as it confirms him in the belief that reduced awareness is the only awareness.*[1]

WHEN WE COME INTO the world, our acquisition of language provides us an understanding through which to interpret our experience. Words, with the exception of personal nouns and pronouns, define the world through the conceptual understanding we share with other members of our language community. Children embrace that foundational understanding, and the interpretation it produces, as certain and absolute rather than the product of judgments and conventions passed on to them by history and culture. Many people continue to hold this foundational understanding as sacred throughout their lives, but now in the 21st century it is difficult to deny the relative nature of the understanding through which we interpret the data of our experience. It may seem natural for some to trust their interpretation and treat it as simply given through the data of the experience, since we do not ordinarily experience a distinction between the data of our experience and the understanding through which we interpret it. Today, however, we know that our experience is a reductive composite, of both the raw data of experience and all of the cultural and linguistic filters within the understanding, through which we interpret that data.

In spite of this, there is a perennial philosophy that is not relative to history, culture, or language community. It is a philosophy, or perhaps better termed an alternative epistemology, that continually claims that pure, unfiltered perception is possible. This alternative epistemology perennially appears in every major religious tradition. In every historical epoch and in every cultural tradition, there are those who practice a form of contemplation that puts them in a position to receive the gift of an unfiltered divine encounter. Unlike those who imagine that they can experience and know God the way they know other things, the contemplative knows that God is encountered in a way very different from any ordinary experience. As we have said, our ordinary experience is always an interpretation based upon the conceptual understanding we bring to the data of the experience. When we encounter the divine, our conceptual understanding is not equipped to do anything but misinterpret that encounter. If we recognize this, we treat our encounters with the divine very differently than our normative experience, and wait upon the divine without all of the filters through which we normally process the data of our experience. Consequently, the divine encounter is something of a pure or direct encounter because there are no appropriate words or concepts through which to interpret it. Maggie Ross refers to the encounter with the divine as "beholding."[2] Beholding is the antithesis of ordinary experience in that the self, which usually processes the data of our experience through an understanding inherited from our history, culture, and language community, is suspended, and we change our focus in order to be open to an engagement that defies whatever understanding we bring to it.

Beholding is an unprocessed engagement that we can never practice, but only prepare for, in order that we might receive the divine encounter as a gift. We do so by focusing away from the self-conscious mind and the ready-made understanding by which it interprets and judges the ordinary data of our experience. What makes the contemplative experience universal and perennial is that contemplatives suspend the understanding through which their minds actively process and assess the data of their experience. If they do not, their God encounters will be quickly interpreted into something that makes sense to their all-too-human understanding. By looking away from themselves and all of the understanding by which they process the data of ordinary experience, they await a knowledge that is given as "pure" gift, and requires nothing of them other than that they wait for it in humble unknowing. This other, alternative epistemology is very different from acquiring knowledge by actively processing, interpreting, testing, and judging the data of our experience.

Unfortunately, most modern minds have been closed to such an alternative epistemology. Indeed, modern science not only insists on a single epistemology but on a single, narrow method as well. Some have even suggested that whatever does not come through that particular method should not be considered knowledge at all. The prejudice of the modern mind is that knowledge must be something that we can possess, but the knowledge that comes from our encounters with the divine possesses us and infuses an ineffable knowing within us. The modern mind believes that only

The contemplative

encounters a God much greater

than our understanding

propositions are truth bearers, but no proposition can bear the truth that comes from our God encounters.

Engagement with the divine is certainly a mystery that defies all the categories of human understanding. The great paradox is that although we know that the mystery is known in a way that our words and understanding can never capture, we continue to search for ever better words to express this mystery that is always beyond our words. Of course, there is a place for words. Without words we can neither record the encounter in our own memory nor encourage others to seek the divine encounter for themselves. As we are forced to use words, however, we must not lose sight, as so many do, that the words we use to record and communicate the encounter are only metaphors for an encounter that is always beyond words. When we take the words too seriously, the encounter becomes something very different from the ineffable engagement we actually beheld. Furthermore, those who only know of such encounters second hand, through words, can all too easily imagine that there are a great many different gods that are being encountered, instead of the same ineffable divinity being expressed in words that are taken too seriously. Since we all too easily mistake the words we use to describe the encounter with the encounter itself, perhaps the best way to express the ineffability of the encounter is *the great silence*.

The words by which we express our God encounters may comfort us and reinforce the lie that we know God as we know other things, but the contemplative knows that God can only be encountered and known in the silent wonder of beholding. All theologies are blasphemous in so far as they attempt to reduce God to something that can be known through the understanding by which we know other things. What the contemplative knows is that the divine is not something that can be reduced to the rank of yet another thing to be known by us. Our understanding is meant to remove the wonder and give us a security in the fact that we know how things work, but the divine is not something that can be known by the mind that we inherit from our history, culture, and language community. We must return to a much more primitive perspective and a more primitive epistemology.

Jesus says, "Truly I tell you, unless you change and become like children, you will never enter the kingdom of heaven."[3] Indeed, only by emptying ourselves of the understanding by which we have been taught to process everything and returning to that pre-linguistic perspective of an infant's wonder, do we open ourselves to a pure encounter with the divine. The acquisition of language, and all the understanding that comes with it, deludes us into believing that we know, and that the wonder of beholding was something to be left behind in our infancy.

There is a great security that comes from believing that we possess knowledge. Our theologies claim to know things about God; when we believe those things we call it faith, but it is a faith in our own understanding rather than a faith in something greater than our understanding. The contemplative encounters a God much greater than our understanding. It is a divinity to be encountered and beheld in wonder rather than one to be known in the way our minds go about knowing other things. The great silence, which is the liminal encounter with the divine, sometimes surprises us, but we can also prepare ourselves to receive the gift of this encounter by turning away from our self-conscious mind and all of the understanding by which it processes all other encounters, and behold the great silence that is God. The prayer of the contemplative is, essentially, an attention to the omnipresence of God. God is omnipresent, not as a theological doctrine, but as the great silence that is present in every moment—but from which we are usually distracted by an overactive mind that refuses to wait in a humble unknowing for a pure wisdom from above.[4] •

NOTES

1 Aldous Huxley, *The Doors of Perception* (London: Chatto & Windus, 1954), 23.

2 Maggie Ross, "Behold not the Cloud of Experience," *The Medieval Mystical Tradition in England VIII*, ed. E.A. Jones (Cambridge: Boydell and Brewer, May 2013).

3 Mt 18:3.

4 Jas 3:17.

The Contemplative Action of Devotion

By Robert Sardello, PhD

I HAVE BEEN EXPLORING contemplative action for a number of years, trying to see how contemplation of any sort has two halves. There is that aspect of entering deeply inward, into the heart, and holding there, in the Silence and in the Stillness, the felt presence of what we contemplate. Contemplation does not have an orientation toward anything outside itself and what we hold therein. We do not contemplate something to try to make something happen in the world. For example, when we contemplate peace, it is not to try and make peace happen. This orientation of soul and spirit does not follow the laws of cause and effect. It follows the laws of oneness, of wholeness, and of a different time than the linearity of clock time. Contemplation occurs within the laws of synchronicity. When we enter into contemplation, the complete soul, spirit, body, earth dimensions of what is held in heart, simultaneously occur in the world, but in mysterious and unexpected ways. Let us explore devotion in the manner of contemplative action.

What is devotion like, when held as an act of contemplation? Devotion is extremely dedicated, unwavering love that is selflessly oriented toward the goodness of another—who may be God, a cause, a profession, a work—really anything, which indicates the great fluidity of devotion that, when entered, opens and fills the interior soul life.

Devotion has real force to it. It is fiery, hot, can be impulsive, and can even seem militant or rash. One thing for sure, we shall have to change our minds about devotion and release any kind of sentimental and pious notions that picture someone quietly praying or exuding a peaceful caring; it may seem that way exteriorly, but the soul is on fire. We have to learn how to hold the fire, how to develop an adequate vessel of soul that can both contain and express the inhering intensity of devotion at the same time.

Without the stabilization of equanimity, it is quite likely that devotion never gets beyond its initial fiery stage, except perhaps in someone with soul qualities like Francis of Assisi. Equanimity concerns the point of balance between efforts we bring to a task and the realization that no matter what we do or how hard we work, what is accomplished is a matter of grace. The capacity to feel the presence of grace, of being graced by the spiritual realms, cools the intense conflagration of devotion to something analogous to a "preboil." If equanimity can be found, the ideal of devotion has a chance of maturing.

Often, in feeling the impulsiveness of desire toward an ideal, the necessary aspect of equanimity is bypassed, leading to an incineration of the soul's initial fire. Devotion is not only the initial dedication but also the finding of inner resources to sustain that initial dedication no matter what. We have to be devoted to devotion itself or it will get lost. Here we enter into the mystical side of the act—devotion is both an act of the soul, and also the inherent spirit presence of the one in whose presence we are. Our devotion is a creative act of the fire of the heart that opens us to the fire of devotion of spirit presences. This "dualitude" (a word to indicate our oneness with what we contemplate and its oneness with us) occurs as a complex unity wherein the amplitude of one aspect intensifies the amplitude of the other, like in kind, as of a spiritual brother or sister. As long as we approach spiritual matters as if they were matters of ordinary consciousness, this mutual awareness cannot be felt, and any burgeoning of devotion lacks the necessary fullness needed to unfold.

Rather than just following our idealism or letting it burn out, it is perhaps important to work at holding in abeyance the object of the ideal and trying to get closer to the fire itself: to get close to the urging itself, as if it were the "angel" of devotion.

Under the conditions of contemplating the presences of devotion itself, the act itself is world-creative. That is, such an "inner" act is not really private and is not confined to being a personal experience. We begin to notice devotion appearing in the world, and there, we can be contemplatively present to other dimensions of its being. Here is an example:

About four years ago, during a time given over to contemplating devotion, I had to have some dental work done in the midst of travel. I was referred to a dentist I did not know. He was a most interesting person. The dental assistant, and even the person taking care of the records, all seemed to exude a kind of radiance; nothing "new age" about it, just a quiet radiance.

This dentist was also very skilled. I noticed that as he was working, pulling one tooth and doing a root canal on another, I did not feel like someone was prying around with a wrench, a hammer, and a screwdriver. Even more interesting, afterward, not only was there no soreness, I actually had more energy.

Let me see if I can describe the actions of the devoted dentist in a way that shows the gesture of devotion. I was not looking around to see if "devotion" was somewhere in the world. Also, I do not think this dentist was deliberately practicing a devotion based upon mental knowledge. His gestures, his actions, his being, the invisible qualities of the space, the way that time unfolded there, were all unified, as if guided by some invisible presence that permeated this situation. I did not look for it, but noticed it happening.

Everything the dentist and the assistants did was completely professional. One certainly could not tell any difference between this office and any other dental clinic. We could not call the practice performed there "alternative dentistry." However, even at the moment of stepping into the waiting room, I felt honored, and honored not merely as a customer. The receptionist spoke in a way that touched the level of soul. No particular content can be pointed to as making what she said any different than any other receptionist. I would say, though, that my soul felt welcomed.

As I waited, the level of anxiety characteristic of such waiting was almost imperceptible. Then the dental assistant called me to the chair. This space was also not different than that of any other dental procedure room. There was, for example, no sweet music being played, nothing external set up to put me into a dreamy state. Once again, though, I did not feel like a car that had just been put into the shop, but like a person, and this was due to the manner of the assistant. There was clearly an interest in me but it was not a feigned interest, nor an interest in the smaller, "ego-me." It was warm interest, focused primarily on why I was there, but it was more than just an interest in the condition of my mouth. It was, rather, that the condition of my mouth, tended in the manner of devotion, was not separated from the whole of my being and, while focused physically, went beyond that.

When the dentist came in to the room, this same quality—though a bit more intense—was also present. He went about his work in a straightforward manner. What most amazed me was that he could be engaged in a series of complex actions while at the same time never losing a presence to the whole of the situation, which included me as a person. I never

We have to be devoted to devotion itself or it will get lost.

for a moment felt myself slipping away and becoming a mouth. He was working with all of me.

The wholeness I felt had to do with a kind of choreography of his actions. "Choreography" is a good word because it approaches describing the manner of his movements that were whole and complete and brought me into the entire action without leaving out any aspect of my being.

The devotion of this dentist consisted of a style of behavior that lived thoughtfully, in and through his body. By saying that he was fully present, I mean that the fullness of his being was brought to the situation. I could see, for example, that he was concerned with whether I was feeling pain. This concern was more than technical, and consisted more of his gestures coming into resonance with mine so that he could actually tell if I was feeling pain before I felt it. Thus, his actions, while remaining completely skilled, were actions acting not on something, but with someone. For him to be able to do this required that he move and act out of a presence to the soul level. His skill and ability also had a kind of "light" about it. What I mean is that being surrounded by drills, tools, strong lights, grinding sounds, metal on tooth, did not have the intensity of being invaded by something "foreign" as it typically would. That element was present, but it had a much lighter feel to it than I had experienced before, as if occurring within a kind of "mystical light." I would say that the technical skills of this dentist were pervaded with the sense that he was engaged in a sacred act with skill rather than merely a technical act.

While we might typically feel that coming upon such a situation, pervaded by devotion, is a lucky accident, what I described above was experienced at a wholly bodily level of being, characterized by a strong feeling of a oneness of spirit, and directly connected as the "other half" of the contemplative engagement with devotion. •

Acts of Compassion,

the Sacramental Imagination, and the Divine Reality Inherent in the World of Things

By Jamie L. Manson, MDiv

I N EARLY DECEMBER 2012, Jennifer Foster, a tourist visiting New York City, took a photo of a police officer helping a homeless man put on a pair of boots. The officer, it turns out, purchased the boots for the man after seeing him barefoot on the street. It was a cold night and the man's feet were badly blistered.

As he knelt before the homeless man to help him put on the new socks and boots, the officer did not know he was being photographed. Foster, who also worked in law enforcement in her home state of Arizona, sent the photo to New York City's Police Department, who then posted it to their official Facebook page.

Within a day or two, the photo was viewed by thousands of people, and the kind NYPD officer was identified as 26-year-old

Larry DePrimo. The photo was reproduced in hundreds of news reports, "liked" on countless Facebook pages, and shared in innumerable Twitter feeds. Within a week's time, the image had been seen by millions on the internet. Judging from the comments they left on blogs and social media sites, most seemed moved deeply by DePrimo's act of generosity.

In a media-saturated culture in which individuals can see as many as 5,000 advertisements a day, it's rare that a single image can give anyone pause, let alone inspire several moments of contemplation. This image, however, reached iconic status, in the true sense of the word. It seemed to have a clarifying effect: helping viewers break through their material attachments and shake off their mundane distractions. It invited them to reconnect with their awareness of what is ultimately meaningful in this life.

Even as religious commitment declines and individualism rises, the reaction to this photo suggested that people around the world still can be moved by the simple act of clothing another human being, or feeding the hungry, or sitting vigil with the sick. Kindness and compassion apparently still touch us at the core of our beings.

More than simply moving us with its generosity, the image, I believe, tapped into our sacramental imagination. It revealed to us that perennial truth that divine reality is inherent in the world of things. Our sacramental imagination allows us to see that the objects, persons, and relationships of our day-to-day life reveal the sacred to us. The idea of a sacramental worldview is based on the belief that, since God is omnibenevolent, or "all-good," there is an intrinsic goodness in all that God creates.

Divine reality is also inherent in the experiences we have with all of creation, be it nature, animals, or other persons. The sacred, therefore, can become present to us through love, forgiveness, compassion, justice, sacrifice, but also in the midst of suffering, brokenness, and desolation. All of these encounters with the holy brim with the opportunity to transform our vision and deepen our awareness of divine reality reaching out to us.

It is the sacramental imagination that gave Dorothy Day the vision to see a prostitute with advanced syphilis as Jesus Christ on her doorstep, and allowed Teilhard de Chardin to see that "Christ has a cosmic body that extends throughout the universe." It is the sacramental view of the world that made Thomas Merton see, on a

It is a sacramental moment, when the God who is love, compassion, and presence becomes incarnate among us.

corner of the shopping district in Louisville, that he was so in love with all of the people buzzing around him; he longed to tell them that "they are all walking around shining like the sun."[1]

However, even the sacramental imagination can have its human limitations.

A curious reporter from *The New York Times* decided to find out the story of the man walking around the streets with those bare feet. When he was located, Jeffrey Hillman proved to be a 54-year-old veteran with two adult children. Also, he was barefoot, yet again.

Hillman explained that, though he was grateful for the gift, he was forced to hide the boots for fear he would be killed by someone attempting to rob him. He also expressed reservations about all of the attention the photo had received, telling the *Times,* "I was put on YouTube. I was put on everything without permission. What do I get?" he said. "This went around the world, and I want a piece of the pie."

With that phrase, the media attention shifted from canonizing a cop to demonizing a destitute man. Many of those viewers, whose sacramental imaginations had been blown open by the image of DePrimo and Hillman, quickly collapsed under feelings of betrayal, disappointment, and even resentment.

"A warm tale turns cold," announced one blogger. A legion of "commenters" unleashed their wrath on Hillman, speculating wildly about all of the ways Hillman had abused DePrimo's gift. "He sold the boots for crack or booze," was the general assessment.

The New York *Daily News* took the investigation a step further, declaring that the man wasn't even homeless. After years of living chronically on the street, Hillman was aided in securing an apartment in the Bronx, which was paid for with Section 8 housing vouchers and Social Security and veteran benefits.

Though I would never presume to say whether Jeffrey Hillman suffers from mental illness or chemical dependency, many women and men who live in conditions similar to his typically do suffer from these afflictions. The image of Hillman's body resting on a sidewalk is a symbol of the deeper injustices that have occurred as the result of decades of failed policies on homelessness.

The sad truth is, though many social service programs are able to secure housing for the homeless, few agencies or charities have adequate resources or staff to offer the level of intensive, long-term support necessary to protect those who suffer with severe mental illness or addiction. Most of the time, it is precisely severe mental illness and addiction that prevent homeless people from receiving the aid they need to live a life that upholds their dignity as human beings.

Of course, our American minds are horrified at the prospect that generous acts could be a waste of our precious time and money. Officer DePrimo's kindness, many will think, ended in failure. We want success. We want results. We want this moment to permanently alter the course of this homeless man's life forever. We want to see the drama of "Amazing Grace" played out before us.

However, such thinking really is antithetical to the sacramental imagination. While it is true that most religious traditions call us to give food, drink, clothing, and shelter to those in need, no tradition that I'm aware of promises that giving these gifts will necessarily lead to the life-changing, "measurable outcomes" we want for those suffering in deprivation. We are only taught that these acts of mercy can lead us to encounter the Divine Reality that is alive within the broken and marginalized.

Most media reports about Officer DePrimo's act focused on his spending $75 of his own money to purchase the socks and boots for Jeffrey Hillman. For me, however, what was most powerful about the image of the cop and the homeless man was that DePrimo got on his knees—literally meeting Jeffrey Hillman where he was—and dared to touch the man's body by helping him put on the new socks and boots.

The photo captures that moment when an act of generosity transforms into a sacred encounter. Jeffrey Hillman sees the God of mercy who dwells within Officer DePrimo, and Officer DePrimo sees the broken, forsaken God who dwells in Jeffrey Hillman.

It is a sacramental moment, when the God who is love, compassion, and presence becomes incarnate among us. The two men participate in divine reality breaking through in this world, and in those moments, all mundane concerns about money, impact, and outcome fade away. Like the sacraments celebrated by religious communities, this sacramental moment will continue to touch the lives of these men, but in ways that will ultimately remain mysterious to us all.

In an interview, Officer DePrimo says he keeps the receipt for the boots inside of his vest to remind him that "sometimes people have it much worse." I hope he will consider keeping that photo in his pocket, too, because it is an icon that expresses the perennial wisdom inherent in all acts of compassion. It is an image that invites us to look courageously into the eyes of human vulnerability, to be fully present even in the most difficult of circumstances, and to take the risk of loving one another, regardless of how it all may turn out. •

NOTES

1 Thomas Merton, *Conjectures of a Guilty Bystander* (New York: Doubleday, 1968).

Paulo Freire
An Unfinished Completed Life

By James D. Kirylo, PhD

Act justly, love tenderly,
and walk humbly with your God. —Micah 6:8

T HE THREE GREAT theological virtues of faith, hope, and love are the collective, transformative prism that necessarily should guide the thinking and action of people of faith. Despite our humanity, with all of its seeming contradictions, our faith journey is not one that is dualistically driven, but one of reconciliation, holistically propelled, that views the God of life as liberator. Moreover, this journey is one that ought to be rooted in humility and authenticity.

Humility is that place that keeps us connected to our everyday-ness, grounds us, maintains our closeness to people, and ultimately "opens our eyes to the presence of God on the earth...."[1] Authentic living implies that our conscious self acts "true," according to our individual self-understanding and the ethical code that we have freely constructed. Thus, the autonomous nature of the concept of authenticity is liberating, in the sense that we live out of choice and commitment as opposed to a sense of duty or obligation.[2]

To that end, our life of "unfinishedness" is one that rests in the warm embrace of Jesus, in our quest of embracing self—while concurrently letting go of self—to live more freely, while simultaneously actively responding to a world in need of voices of conscience calling out oppressive structures, practices, and attitudes that keep humanity from being fully liberated.

When I reflect on a person who lived his life rooted in the theological virtues, yet at the same time authentically lived, humbly walked, and actively responded, my mind is immediately drawn to Paulo Freire, the Brazilian existential thinker, educator, and philosopher. With an insatiable desire to learn from the beginning to the end of his life, Freire understood himself as a human being thoughtfully under construction, continuously reinventing his life and work. In that light, he saw life as something that was not predetermined and was intensely aware of his unfinishedness; he believed that to remain static was not an option.[3]

Particularly among those in the field of education, Freire is recognized on the same plateau as John Dewey, Lev Vygotsky, Maria Montessori and others. He is unequivocally one of the most important progressive educators the world has seen in the last one hundred years. He is acclaimed as the initial protagonist for what is known as "critical pedagogy" which, in short, is an approach to education that provides perceptive insight for understanding dehumanizing structures, practices, and attitudes.[4] Much can naturally be discussed regarding Freire's work related to critical pedagogy; however, it is my aim here to succinctly spotlight the activeness of his faith and what it may teach us as we each navigate our faith journey of unfinishedness.

Freire's thought and action was particularly filtered through his Christian faith, motivating and challenging him, particularly as it related to promoting human rights. For Freire, this meant never submitting to the notion that "things are as they are because they cannot be any other way." That is, he understood God to be a real presence in history, yet this presence did not imply that human beings could not be partakers in making history, but possessed the possibility to transform the world and free it from human exploitation.[5]

Freire's belief system, therefore, was not driven by a fatalistic perspective whereby, if something may not have gone his way (for example, the hunger crises he faced as a child), he would have reduced the failure or misfortune to simply "God's will." This is no small matter, particularly in light of the cultural context of his era; for many during that time (and remnants of this thinking still exist today), misfortune and poverty were somehow a part of God's grand plan and test. Also, the "encouragement" from the religious establishment was that people should simply "offer" their misery up to God and their reward would come, soon enough, in the afterlife. This type of thinking is rooted in a colonial legacy, or in what Freire characterizes as the "traditionalist church" which, in its worst manifestation, focused on "winning" souls, often through masochistic threats, emphasizing that the more one suffers, the more one is purified in achieving eternal salvation.[6]

This point of view so conditioned the masses in his native Brazil that it was extraordinarily difficult for them to see the historical contextualization of the reasons for their abject poverty. That is, they were made blind to the reality that their victimization was perpetrated by a political-religious-social structural system that was human-generated, and not something that was in the design of God's plan. Consequently, the people's inability to "act" in history, and their understanding of a God who acts in history, was a great challenge for Freire while doing his pedagogical-political work. For the dominant group (many in the hierarchal church, landowners, and those in political power), the traditionalist point of view of the Church naturally suited them well because it maintained the status quo, preserving their comfortable living conditions.[7]

"...re-create the world, not for my brothers' domination but for their liberation."

Freire's view of Christ as the incarnate word was one of relationship; to teach the Gospel is not only to have experienced the message, but also to live and personify it.[8] He rejected the gross misrepresentation of a Christianity that was exploitive and dehumanizing. Rather, he undoubtedly was attuned to the Exodus story, and took seriously Jesus' proclamation with which he first began his public ministry (Lk 4:18-19). In short, Freire possessed a deep friendship with the living Christ and saw the God of life as liberator, setting free those living in inhumane and unjust circumstances. For Freire, reading the Word of God and putting it into practice necessarily invites one "to re-create the world, not for my brothers' domination but for their liberation."[9]

In that light, a church that critically analyzes inequitable social structures, denounces oppression and announces institutional change and radical transformation, and concretely acts on behalf of those who have been historically marginalized, is one that Freire characterizes as the prophetic church, a more authentic expression of the Gospel message.[10] Freire remained unwavering in his life's work, cultivating the betterment of humanity where, ultimately, oppressive forces would no longer have their way. In the spirit of the perennial tradition and influenced by the optimism of Emmanuel Mounier, who emphasized making visible in practice the spiritual nature of God in humanizing humanity, Freire understood the importance of the vision of a more just world, a more democratic society, a place that would celebrate differences, and a people who would live among each other in respect, love, and freedom.

In the final analysis, Paulo Freire's deep spirituality and his theological perspective significantly contributed to the development of liberation theology which, at its core, views the world through the eyes of the poor, or through what Ignacio Ellacuría calls the crucified people.[11]

While Freire left this earth years ago, his unfinished completed life continues to inspire many of us to "act justly, love tenderly, and walk humbly with [our] God" (Mi 6:8). •

NOTES

1 H.J.M. Nouwen, *Gracias: A Latin American Journal* (New York: Orbis Books, 1983), 162.

2 According to Martin Heidegger, life lived inauthentically ultimately leads to anxiety, despair, and meaninglessness (Martin Heidegger, *Being and Time* (Albany, NY: State University of New York Press, 1996). In other words, authentic living liberates us from a contrived filtering of our interpretation and meaning of the world through institutional or other external constructs, as opposed to authentically exploring meaning through existential experiences (Ibid; also Abraham Maslow, *Toward a Psychology of Being*, 2nd Ed. (Princeton, NJ: Van Nostrand, 1968)).

3 Paulo Freire, *Daring to Dream: Toward a Pedagogy of the Unfinished*, trans Alexandre K. Oliveira (Boulder, CO: Paradigm Publishers, 2007); Paulo Freire, *Pedagogy of Freedom: Ethics, Democracy, and Civic Courage* (Lanham, MD: Rowman and Littlefield Publishers, Inc., 1998).

4 Peter McLaren, *Che Guevara, Paulo Freire, and the Pedagogy of Revolution* (Lanham, MD: Rowman & Littlefield Publishers, Inc., 2000); J. L. Kincheloe, "Afterward: Ten Short Years — Acting on Freire's Requests," *Journal of Thought*, 43 (1&2, 2008, Spring–Summer), 163–171.

5 Paulo Freire, *Pedagogy of the Heart* (New York: Continuum, 1998), 104.

6 Paulo Freire, *Letters to Cristina: Reflections on my Life and Work*, trans D. Macedo with Q. Macedo and A. Oliveira (New York: Routledge, 1996); Paulo Freire, *The Politics of Education: Culture, Power, and Liberation* (New York: Bergin & Garvey, 1985).

7 Paulo Freire, *The Politics of Education*; Paulo Freire, in J.W. Donohue, "Paulo Freire — Philosopher of Adult Education," *America*, CXXVII (7, 1972), 167–170.

8 Paulo Freire, in W.B. Kennedy, "Conversation with Paulo Freire," *Religious Education*, 79 (4, Fall 1984), 511–522; Paulo Freire, "Know, Practice, and Teach the Gospels," *Religious Education*, 79 (4, Fall 1984), 547–548.

9 Paulo Freire, "Letter to a Theology Student," *The Catholic Mind*, LXX (No. 1265, 1972), 6–8.

10 Paulo Freire, *The Politics of Education*.

11 Michael E. Lee, *Bearing the Weight of Salvation: The Soteriology of Ignacio Ellacuría* (New York: Crossroad, 2009).

A San Andreas Fault in the Country of the Heart

By Cynthia Bourgeault, PhD

O PEN ANY TEXTBOOK on Christian spirituality or mysticism and you will find the perennial philosophy prominently represented: from the Christian Neoplatonism of Origen to the sixth century writings of Pseudo Dionysius that so profoundly impacted the mysticism of the West, to the imagery of the ladder popularized by John Climacus in the seventh century which framed the monastic praxis of both Christian East and Christian West. Given the sheer weight of spiritual authority behind this roadmap, Christian orthodoxy has always, somewhat perversely, rested uneasily within it. That is not to say the perennial philosophy has been without influence in Christianity; it has in fact exerted enormous influence. It takes a well-practiced theological eye to spot the San

Andreas Fault running through this magnificent body of spiritual teaching. Yet the fault line is there, and once you see it, a lot of the early history of Christianity makes a good deal more sense. I am not talking here about those obvious theological conundrums such as Augustine's "grace versus works" but something much more fundamental: an uneasy intuition, just below the surface of the collective theological imagination, that there is something fundamentally askew in the metaphysics themselves.

COSMOLOGICAL REDSHIFT

As I SEE IT, there are three core metaphysical building blocks of the perennial philosophy. The first is what I call a "cosmological redshift." Redshift (alias the "Doppler effect") is a basic law of physics stating that as soundwaves or lightwaves move away from their source, their wavelength appears to lengthen, moving toward the "red" end of the visible spectrum—or, with soundwaves, to a slower vibration. That's why the ambulance siren drops to a lower pitch as the ambulance hurtles past you and on down the street.

From its point of origin in a hypothetical "big bang," the universe hurtling out through time and space has steadily lost energy, grown colder and more dense. The molten energy of that initial explosion gradually "cooled off" to become quarks, particles, atoms, molecules, rocks, cells, amoebas, people. In a redshift universe, as energy travels outward from the source, its frequency diminishes. Things grow more solid, cooler, less like the source itself.

Interestingly, that's exactly what the perennial philosophy has been saying all along as well—only it has been saying it in the realm of spiritual, rather than scientific, cosmology. Underlying that great hierarchical procession of realms traditionally known as the "great chain of being," it is not hard to spot as the real operative principle. With the Godhead, or Source, envisioned as the initial "big bang" of the great chain of being, creation inevitably presents itself as a *descent*—a vast cosmic Doppler effect. The "energies" of the Godhead stream outward, losing frequency in the process and giving rise to a series of embedded universes, each one progressively more dense and coarse than its predecessor.

Here the basic cosmic principle, both energetically and morally, is that to be created—particularly as a flesh-and-blood human being—means to descend to a lower state, a more coarse and "corrupt" mode of being, subject to the laws of entropy and decay. So it follows inevitably that the return to God must entail some form of *ascent*: working one's way back up the ray of creation like a salmon working its way upstream.

THE CORRUPTION OF MATTER

I**T IS ONLY** in the past century that we have come to understand definitively that spirit and matter are not fundamentally different. Thanks to Einstein, we now know that matter is merely a more condensed form of energy, and what we have traditionally called "spirit" would presumably be merely a much more subtle form of energy. However, until the beginning of the twentieth century (a mere drop in the bucket of the overall lifespan of the perennial philosophy) that continuum was unsuspected, and in the pervasively redshift modality of traditional Wisdom metaphysics, there is a virtually unanimous tendency to identify density as the opponent of spirit and the root cause of all human misery. The very density which confers our human form (traditionally known as "flesh") is seen as the primary corruption that must be overcome in order to reclaim our true spiritual identity. Along with a tendency to regard matter (density) as the primary source of our human exile comes the tendency to identify God with the top of the great chain of being only, not with the whole chain.

SPIRITUALIZATION AS ASCENT

G**IVEN THESE FIRST** two tenets, the third follows inescapably. If we have "fallen" into matter and density, then the way home must inevitably entail an ascent. Since, in the spiritual realm as well as the material one, to ascend requires energy, most spiritual technologies in the classic Wisdom traditions are built on some form of "conservation of energy." Through celibacy, meditation, recollection, attention, one "collects" and "deepens" the reserve of energy so that spirit can rise to its home in Spirit.

ROM THIS EXPLORATION it is not hard to see where the fundamental points of tension will arise in Christianity. First, and most significant, the tendency to equate physical density with corruption and to picture the journey to God as an ascent to a more spiritualized plane of reality directly clashes with that foundational datum of Christian lived experience: that in Jesus, God had drawn very close and, in fact, "became flesh and dwelt among us" (Jn 1:14). At the very epicenter of Christian identity—in direct challenge to the perennial roadmap—is the lived experience that *God does not lose energy by plunging into form.* If anything, the thrust is in the opposite direction, toward a kind of spiritual "blueshift" in which Jesus, like a great magnifying glass, makes more concentrated and vivid the accessible presence of Divine Spirit itself. While Christianity has often lost its nerve around extending this "magnifying" capacity to anyone other than Jesus himself, still, the core theological proclamation at stake in the statement "God was in Christ reconciling the world to himself" (2 Cor 5:19) is that God can be fully present in the physical world without form being an impediment to divinity—or, to put it another way, that things do not lose spirit simply because they inhabit form. This "blueshift" modality of Christian lived experience is in direct tension to the "redshift" thrust of the grand perennial roadmap. Even more against the metaphysical grain is that stunning Johannine intimation that the reason for Jesus' mission is that "God so loved the world" (Jn 3:16). There is something more than just a rescue operation going on here; the created world is infinitely precious and valuable in its own right.

Following from this intuition then—and in contrast to the dominant upward thrust of the perennial roadmap—is that corollary tenet, again rooted in lived Christian experience, that the way to God is not up but down. The essence of this intuition is brilliantly expressed in that great Pauline hymn of Philippians 2:6-11, which captures in a highly condensed and compelling form the energy field pervading the entire gospel tradition. At the very heart of that original Christian vision, tugging against the Neoplatonic undercurrents that would eventually overwhelm it, is the staunch intuition that the Jesus mystery is ultimately not about ascent but descent; its epicenter lies in *kenosis*, self-emptying:

Though his state was that of God,
Yet he did not claim equality with God
Something he should cling to.

Rather, he emptied himself[1]
And assuming the state of a slave,
He was born in human likeness.

He being known as one of us
Humbled himself obedient unto death
Even death on a cross

For this God raised him on high
And bestowed on him the name
Which is above every other name.

So that at the name of Jesus
Every knee should bend
In heaven, on earth, and under the earth,

And so every tongue should proclaim
"Jesus Christ is Lord!"
To God the Father's Glory.

Theologians have had a heyday with this passage, of course, emphasizing the spiritual virtues of humility and obedience, but *metaphysically* it again reinforces that counterintuitive wisdom that one does not lose force or Godhood—one does not move away from God—by entering the realm of form; quite to the contrary, *descent* seems to be the chief operative in making the fullness of the divine manifestation happen.

Thus two areas of direct collision leave Christianity in fundamental quandary about its metaphysical underpinnings. Perhaps that is the meaning of Jesus' cryptic warning in Luke 12:52 (and the Gospel of Thomas 16) that "the household will be divided, three against two and two against three." A basically ternary theology erected on the foundations of a binary metaphysics is bound to result in cognitive dissonance. While this dissonance is never named for what it is, it makes its presence known in those periodic

...we have come to understand definitively that spirit and matter are not fundamentally different.

theological upheavals and course corrections that so dominate the early centuries of Christian history.

I was particularly gratified to see Fr. Bruno Barnhart, in his recent book *The Future of Wisdom*, finally naming this issue that has been for so long the unmentionable elephant in the parlor. In a section detailing "The Limitations of Monastic Wisdom"—or, in other words, influences that have pulled the innate Christian sapiential compass off course—he specifically flags "a very strong Platonic influence which supports the vertical and interiorizing monastic options and sanctions an ascending crystal tower of spiritual theology."[2]

Many people still like to think of metaphysics as an objective science—true everywhere, and for all times—rather than the art of selectively choosing the "right view" (as the Buddhists call it): the pattern that best highlights and unifies the lived reality of a particular faith tradition. I run into this prejudice all the time in my own work with attempting to reclaim an authentic Christian Wisdom tradition. It is remarkable how many people assume that since I am using the word "Wisdom," I am teaching perennial philosophy metaphysics. This assumption leads many of my more "spiritual but not religious" acquaintances to expect that I have simply dispensed with the cranky eccentricities of Christian theology and found my Wisdom ground in the "transcendent unity of religions."[3] It has led many more traditionally minded Christians to dismiss my work out of hand as "gnostic." Both of these assumptions are equally untrue.

The transcendent unity of religions notwithstanding, in Christianity, for better or worse, we are dealing with a horse of a different metaphysical color. Throughout those early centuries of Christian identity formation, it seems that the early Church Fathers could generally smell ternary metaphysics even if they couldn't articulate it. While Patristic thinkers such as Iranaeus and Tertullian are highly in disfavor nowadays because of their relentless fulminations against heresy, it must be admitted that these early Christian patriarchs did have a strong intuitive grasp of where the metaphysical center of gravity really lay in Christianity and a sixth sense for when Christianity was wandering off its metaphysical course. Over the centuries—from those early polemicists of the second and third centuries down through the medieval inquisitors and papal bulls of more recent eras—institutional Christianity has proved itself more than willing to disown and condemn even its loftiest mystical expressions and most profound non-dual teachings rather than run the risk of having the entire theological structure compromised by a metaphysical framework intuitively sensed to be alien. It is a kind of brute, intuitive courage, not pretty in its own right, but validly expressing an intimation of something here too precious to lose. Named as "ternary metaphysics," we can perhaps finally see it with less heat and more light. •

This article is adapted from Cynthia Bourgeault's forthcoming book, The Holy Trinity and the Law of Three, *which will be published by Shambhala Publications in July 2013.*

NOTES

1 In Greek, the word being translated as "to empty oneself" is *kenosein*, hence the derivation of the term *kenosis*.
2 Bruno Barnhart, *The Future of Wisdom: Toward a Rebirth of Sapiential Christianity* (New York: Continuum, 2008), 12.
3 This term was coined by contemporary Traditionalist metaphysician Frithjof Schuon. See Schuon, *The Transcendent Unity of Religions* (New York: Harper and Row, 1974).

Epilogue

By James Finley, PhD

A MAGICIAN FANS OUT a deck of cards face down on a table and says, "Go ahead; pick a card, any card." It does not matter which card you choose, and then bury facedown, back into the deck. The magician will, inexplicably, bring it forth from your shirt pocket or, perhaps, from behind your ear.

Now imagine you are out walking on the beach and God says, "Go ahead, pick a grain of sand, any grain." No matter what grain of sand you choose, God is present in it. Since God is not subject to division or diminishment of any kind, God is completely present in that one little grain of sand. Furthermore, since the whole universe flows from God, is sustained by God and subsists in God, you are holding in your hand a grain of sand in which you, along with the whole universe and everyone and everything in it, is wholly present.

Surprised by such an all-encompassing oneness, you begin to get a little weak in the knees. Then God moves in to finish you off by suddenly expanding this awareness of realized oneness in all directions. "Go ahead," God says, "pick a place, a situation, a circumstance in which you might find yourself." If you choose a wooded area, you see yourself in your mind's eye surrounded by trees. God is there, inviting you to reach out and pick a leaf off one of the low-hanging branches. As you do so, you realize you are holding a leaf in which the totality of reality is wholly present. If you choose your own home, God is there, inviting you to choose something, anything at all: the teakettle on the stove, or perhaps a chair in a corner of the living room. No matter what you might choose, you realize you are choosing something in which God is wholly present, loving you, and all people and all things, into being.

Then God invites you to reflect on any aspect of yourself. No matter what aspect of yourself you focus on, God is there, wholly present in each breath, each thought and feeling, each turn of your head. You realize, as you sit, that God is present as the ungraspable immediacy of your sitting. As you stand, God is there as the ungraspable immediacy of your standing. As you laugh, God is there as your laughter. As you cry, God is wholly present in each tear that falls from your eyes.

It does not matter what little thing you might choose, within or around you. It might just be the thing that awakens you from your fitful dream of being separate from God, who is the reality of yourself and all that is real. May each of us be so fortunate as to be overtaken by God in the midst of little things. May we each be so blessed as to be finished off by God, swooping down from above or welling up from beneath, to extinguish the illusion of separateness that perpetuates our fears. May we, in having our illusory, separate self slain by God, be born into a new and true awareness of who we really are: one with God forever. May we continue on in this true awareness, seeing in each and every little thing we see, the fullness of God's presence in our lives. May we also be someone in whose presence others are better able to recognize God's presence in their lives, so that they, too, might know the freedom of the children of God. •

This article is the epilogue to the manuscript of a book currently being written by James Finley, titled Little Things that Fill the Whole World: Gospel Metaphors of Spiritual Awakening.

Center for
Action and
Contemplation

Home of THE ROHR INSTITUTE

A collision of opposites forms the cross of Christ.
One leads downward preferring the truth of the humble.
The other moves leftward against the grain.
But all are wrapped safely inside a hidden harmony:
One world, God's cosmos, a benevolent universe.